LONG RANGE PLANNING

A How-To-Do-It Manual
For Public Libraries

Suzanne W. Bremer

*HOW-TO-DO-IT MANUALS
FOR LIBRARIANS*

Number 40

NEAL-SCHUMAN PUBLISHERS, INC.
New York London

Published by Neal-Schuman Publishers, Inc.
100 Varick Street
New York, NY 10013

Printed and bound in the United States of America

Library of Congress Cataloging-in-Publication Data

Bremer, Suzanne W.
    Long range planning : a How-to-do-it manual for public librarians
/ Suzanne W. Bremer.
        p.   cm.
    Includes bibliographical references and index.
    ISBN 1-55570-162-0 : $39.95
    1. Library planning--United States.   I.   Title.
Z678.B817 1994
027.073 --dc20
                                                    94-5841
                                                    CIP

TO WLF AND EWB, WHO TAUGHT ME THAT THE FIRST STEP IN SOLVING ANY PROBLEM IS TO GET A CLEAN PAD OF PAPER—SWB

CONTENTS

ACKNOWLEDGMENTS

To Suzanne B. Fleischmann for funding it.
To Susan M. Palmatier for inspiring it.
To Elizabeth Futus for suggesting it.
To Jane V. Peyrouse for living with it.

INTRODUCTION

No one book can contain all you need to know to create a successful long range plan for your library. Libraries are complex places with no two alike, and an endless stream of variables—constituencies served, funding mechanisms, space requirements, and so on.

Planning for the future implies a certain optimism that, if nothing else, there will be a tomorrow. Without a plan, tomorrows keep coming, but the future never seems to arrive.

This manual is primarily intended for public library directors, trustees, and staff. School and special libraries will find much that can be adopted to fit their circumstances.

Since no one book can contain all you need to know about planning, most chapters include a list of suggested readings. *Please read these books and articles as you go through the planning process.* You may want to assign a selection or two to each member of the planning committee, rather than having everyone read all the articles.

Throughout the manual, the Danville Public Library (DPL) is offered as an example. Danville, at least as it is described here, does not exist. Rather the Danville Library is a composite. It could be any public library where the folks who run it have decided to commit their time and resources toward creating a plan that works for them.

Make no mistake, making a long range plan for a library requires much thought, discussion, and just plain hard work. There may be disagreements, compromise may be required, or people may have to change the way they think about the library. But, if approached with a spirit of adventure, planning becomes far less arduous. Here is the chance to explore the library's future, to seek new ways to better serve the community, to seize the day.

Planning by itself doesn't make it happen. It is possible to work your way slowly and carefully through the planning process, write a wonderful plan, and then have none of it happen. Planning is like a lot of toys—batteries are not included. After the plan is made, it takes still more work to make it happen at the library.

Use the planning process to generate the goodwill that you will need to actually carry out the plan. Ask for people's opinions, advice, ideas, and suggestions. Tell them what you are doing. Talk about what you want the library to become. Look for clues. Listen for answers.

1 THE PLANNING PROCESS

Planning is a dynamic process. It is an attempt, based on inquiry and evaluation, to anticipate the future. A plan is, at best, an educated guess. So why take up the time consuming task of creating a formal, long range plan, especially at a public library where, more likely than not, "we're just treading water trying to stay afloat"? Public libraries exist in a very competitive environment. Funding is often hard to come by. Materials costs are raising exponentially; the body of materials from which to select has grown geometrically; patrons have rising expectations.

The information age is becoming a reality. Personal computers, modems, videos, and compact discs are powerful information storage and retrieval technologies. How will libraries, well versed in the older information technologies such as books, magazines, indexes, anthologies, and encyclopedias, adapt to the new, electronic formats?

These information technologies have brought about a landslide of data, sounds, and images that people—our users—alternately absorb and deflect. Fifty years ago, information moved at the speed of sound, now it travels at the speed of light. We live in a world in which, as it is happening, we watch a witness testify before the Senate committee, or the Marines wade ashore. With all this flashy, neon-colored media in the world, people need help sorting it all out, separating the wheat ("To thine own self be true . . .") from the chaff (Elvis spotted at the 7-11).

WHY PLAN?

Embedded in the public library movement is the belief that people have a fundamental right to know. No matter how rich you are, how old you are, where you come from, or where you call home, you have a right to both information and knowledge. In 1982, to honor public libraries, the Post Office issued a commemorative stamp. The stamp proclaimed "America's Libraries Legacies to Mankind."[1] While this may sound a bit overblown, it is in fact a guiding principle. Public libraries offer entertainment, education, and illumination to all who come through the doors. The trouble is in keeping the doors open.

The aim of creating a formal, long range plan in a public library is to develop, in a fair and systematic manner. Planning is a chance to inquire and investigate, to examine your library, the services that it offers, and the community that it serves, and then to envision the future and the steps that need to be taken to arrive there. Without a plan, the library's future will unfold in a more or less random manner. With a plan, those that lead the library have a way to direct efforts and evaluate opportunities.

This manual is not an oracle so much as a starting point. By no means does it contain "the answer." There is no one right answer for your library. Rather, there are tools and techniques that allow you to explore your current situation and the options that are open to you. The steps outlined here, and in other sources, are ways to begin the discussion. No one is better qualified than you, the library director, staff, trustee, and planning committee members, to plot your library's future. You are in a position to know your community and its needs, and the library and how it might meet those needs.

PLANNING IS NOT A QUICK FIX

A formal, long range, thoughtful plan requires a full year to create. Achieving the objectives listed in the plan may take from five to ten years. Realizing a goal may take decades. For a plan to be successful, it must be allowed time to work.

Most libraries write plans that cover a five-year period. This allows enough time to achieve some idealistic goals, but is a short enough time frame so as to be realistic. There may be a reason to create a plan that spans a longer or shorter time. A new librarian, who has yet to assimilate the nuances of the community, may be more comfortable with a three-year plan. A library that has just completed extensive building renovations may be at a point where it is appropriate to spend the next eight years focused on building library services.

PLANS CAN BE CHANGED

At times, you may have no alternative but to change your plans. If none of the proposed funding becomes available, then ground breaking for the library's addition will have to be postponed. The objectives targeted for year three will have to be put off until years four or five. When presented with a budget cut, the librarian can point to the plan and say to the budget committee, "That cut means that we can't do this, and we'll be doing a lot less of that."

A plan can be used to measure and evaluate opportunities that present themselves. If, at the reading of a will, it is discovered that the library has been left a little something, the plan can be moved forward (e.g., year four's objectives could be met in years two and three, we can buy a computer this year instead of next.) A plan not only helps to keep things moving forward, but, as time passes you can gauge the effectiveness of your efforts. Also, a formal plan makes it hard to accuse the library of being capricious or frivolous.

Early in the planning process, set up a timetable for the planning committee to follow. Under most circumstances it takes a year to complete the planning process. By shortening the time allotted, you may not allow for enough discussion, reflection, and consensus building. By taking longer than a year, you run the risk of losing momentum and being considered "all talk." Use timetables and deadlines to keep the discussions moving forward.

As shown in the sample timetable (Figure 1-1), several steps in the process will go on simultaneously. The results of the inventory may not be complete when the planning committee begins to draft the library's mission statement; the mission statement will still be under discussion when the committee starts to examine the roles played by the library.

PLANNING IS CYCLICAL

After completing the plan, the library puts it into action, doing all (or almost all) of the activities that the plan calls for while meeting the goals targeted by the planning committee. As time passes, the library reviews the results of its efforts and modifies its activities, thereby raising or lowering expectations and adopting to change. As the library approaches the completion of the activities called for in the plan, it will have to start the next round of planning. Four to six years after the first plan is written, it will be time to convene another planning committee, take inventory, discuss the library's mission, roles, goals, and objectives all over again.

When setting up your planning schedule, coordinate the process so completed plan will have an impact on the town's budget cycle. Issuing the library's plan in February allows for discussion, reaction, and the continued building of support before the first meeting of the budget committee in April.

FIGURE 1-1: **Danville Public Library Planning Timetable**

Danville Public Library Planning Timetable

Danville Public Library Planning Timetable

Planning Stage	Mar	April	May	June	July	Aug	Sept	Oct	Nov	Dec	Jan	Feb	Mar
Recruit Planning Committee	X												
1st Committee Meeting		X											
Taking Inventory			X	X	X								
Draft Mission Statement				X	X	X							
Select Roles						X	X	X					
Formulate Goals & Objectives								X	X				
Action Plan & Review										X	X		
Write & Distribute												X	X

Other Timing Considerations

1) Town budget hearings start in April. The plan will be in circulation by the end of March.

2) In house user statistics will be gathered early in May, to avoid the influence of "end-of-school-itis" as the high school seniors rush to the library to complete their English theses.

Notes:

_____

_____

_____

_____

_____

_____

FIGURE 1-2: The Planning Cycle

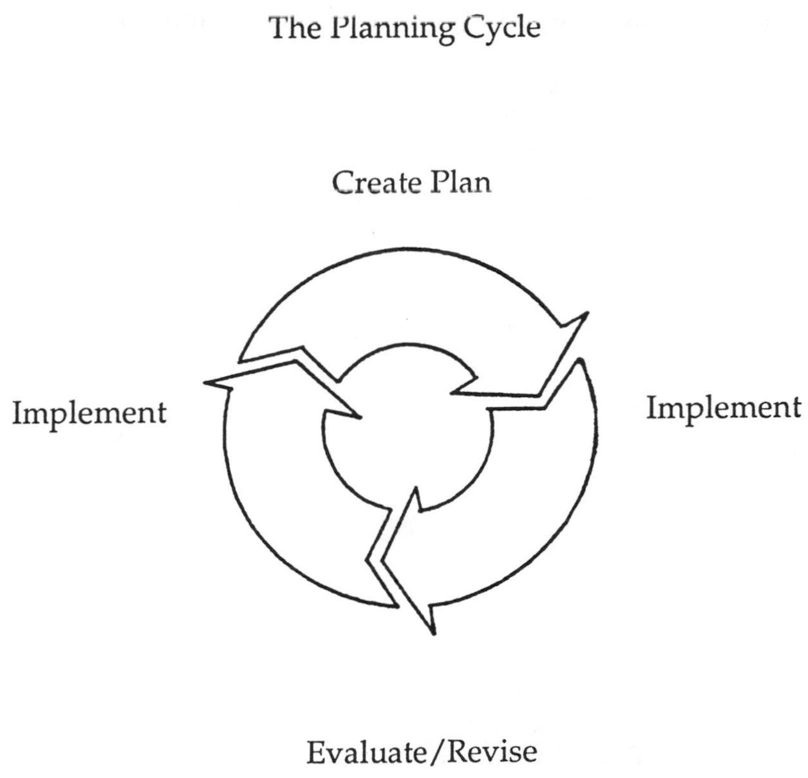

The Planning Cycle

Create Plan

Implement   Implement

Evaluate/Revise

Another cycle to keep in mind is the economic cycle. Is your community in the middle of good times or bad? The state of the local economy will not only determine the level of funding that the library can realistically expect, it may influence the roles that the library plays. Chances are, when the times are good, folks might be more interested in building the addition to the library. When the factory lays off another shift, the library needs to recognize helping townspeople survive as its primary goal. Information on job hunting, social services, and how to stretch your food dollar by growing a victory garden are needed more than lectures on early-American silversmithing.

Sometimes libraries undertake long range planning with a specific project already in mind; these are often automation or building related projects. In the early stages of the planning process, set these assumptions aside. See if you can arrive at the need for a computer assumptions aside. See if you can arrive at the need for a computer upgrade or building renovations by a different route. The library needs an addition not because the librarian and the trustees want one, but because, in order to meet our objective of expanded services to children, we must have a children's room.

How ambitious should the plan be? How high should your library aim? While there is nothing wrong with modest intentions, nothing was ever gained by half measures. Find a balance. You should be reasonably sure that you can deliver on your promises. The library should reflect both your town's expectations and aspirations. In some sections of the plan, stretch what is possible to the limits. In other areas, more modest objectives may be appropriate.

Beware of building expectations on technologies that do not yet exist. Be extremely wary of being the test site for a new computer system (this is known as being a beta site). Much can, and often does, go wrong in the development of hardware and software. Sometimes what seems like a reasonable use of computers on the drawing board, in fact turns out to be less efficient than the "old fashion" manual method. As a general rule, rely on proven technologies, not promises.

PLANNING CREATES PRIORITIES

Some activities, programs, and services are more important than other activities, programs, and services. When some things are more important, other things become less important. Restoration of the library's much loved collection of stuffed birds may be far less important than the renovation of the reading room. This may upset those who really like the stuffed birds ("Why it just won't be the library without the birds!"). But the impact of the stuffed bird advocates can be minimized if you have carefully and fairly considered all points of view, and can show that your plan provides for the greater common good.

Just because something is relatively unimportant, doesn't always mean that it can be ignored. A complete plan must include provisions for the less important priorities. Because their restoration doesn't have a high priority at the library, the stuffed birds might be donated to the high school science department.

A library has three types of resources that it can allocate—time, people, and money. While money may often seem the most important of the three, people can be used to go look for money. If they keep at it, even the most understaffed library will eventually complete a project. Be careful when budgeting people where time and money are lacking. People are at once the most fragile and the most marvelous resource. If folks didn't show up to work at the library every day to work at the circulation desk or in the technical services department, the place couldn't function. A dissatisfied or half-hearted staff member can quickly sink even the best funded program. Ask for their comments, questions, and suggestions not just during the planning process but regularly in the course of running the library.

In the long run, it is less expensive to do something right the first time. There is nothing more heartbreaking than a library that has to fill in the foundation for the addition because the key piece of funding that everyone was so sure would be voted in didn't come through. Spending the extra money for full MARC (Machine Readable Cataloging) records may seem like a lot of bother, but when upgrading a circulation system you may discover those nonstandard bibliographic records were a false economy.

DON'T FIGHT OVER CHEAP SEATS!

Sometimes, when watching people run a race you may notice a remarkable phenomenon. Two runners, way back in the pack, with only a marginal chance of winning, will start to duel one another. They'll run hard, knocking themselves out over twelfth place. You wonder why one of the runners doesn't point to the runner who is leading the race and yell out to his fellow duelist, "Forget this! Let's go after first place!" Even if you fail to win the blue ribbon, fourth and fifth places are better than twelfth and thirteenth places everytime. In public funding budget battles, the library and the schools may be pitted against each other, fighting over second to last place. They're fighting over cheap seats while the police or fire department walk off with the cake. A more productive approach would be for the school and the library to band together and coordinate their efforts. Together they could broadcast the message that education is essential to the community's economic future.

While some may be indifferent about what you are doing, many people have deep and earnest feelings about their library. It may be difficult, especially if you have been associated with the library for some time, to listen to those unfamiliar with the library "spout off." Listen to all points of view. Even the longest, most rambling diatribe may contain a kernel of truth, legitimate complaint, or suggestion. Try to be as objective as possible. Involve as many people as you can—talk to users, nonusers, people that you meet socially, over brown bags at lunch—ask them what they like about the library and what they don't like, ask if they would prefer longer summer hours or another story hour each week. This kind of dialog should go on all the time, not just during the inventory segment of the planning cycle. Trustees, staff members, and Friends of the Library, as well as the Library Director, should be looking for comments.

STUDY OTHER LIBRARIES AS EXAMPLES

Talk with the directors, trustees, staffers, and users of other local libraries. (State and regional library association conventions are outstanding settings for exchanging shop talk.) Contrast and compare your library's experience and situation with that of other libraries. When someone else has a resounding success or a smashing failure, ask yourself "Can we do something like that?" or "How can we avoid that?" Don't dismiss what happens at different-sized libraries, or at different-types of libraries. Whether academic, corporate, medical, large and metropolitan, or small and rural, all libraries do essentially the same things. All libraries anticipating the user's needs and identify materials that meet those needs. They then acquire, process, distribute, track, store, and make available to their users that material. Follow the goings on in the larger public libraries by reading the professional journals. *Library Journal* is an excellent place to start.

Contrast and compare is a good technique to use when starting and guiding a group discussion. How is this type of patron different from that type of patron? How are they the same? How will the new computer system be different from the system that we use now? These little bits of information are like tiles in a mosaic—they can be used to put together a picture of your library.

Just as all libraries are the same in the abstract, in the details each individual library is unique. The constituency that it serves, the programs and the collections that it offers, and the history that has brought it to this point vary from one library to even its closest peer. Each library is different. The mix of the variables listed above, the library's relationship with the agencies that authorize and govern it (aldermen, mayors, town managers, boards of trustees), the patchwork of federal, state, and local funding, and the grants, gifts, and endowments that keep the doors open mean that each library's plan must be custom made. There is no one formula for success. Rather, a successful library is characterized by an ability to balance experimentation with continuity.

EXPERIMENT

Try different things. If it works, great! If not, move on and try something else. Learn from your mistakes and don't worry about assigning blame. When something works (and since you're trying a lot of things, a couple of them are bound to be wildly successful) continue it. If the book sale is popular, do it again next year. If there was standing room only at the job searching workshop, offer it again and add additional workshops on resume writing and interview skills. Follow up on successes.

When something is successful, stop and ask yourself what went right. While good fortune often seems to be a deciding factor, timing, imagination, preparation, clear communication, hard work, and the right mix of people are the real elements of a successful venture.

There is a tendency to try to solve problems too early in the planning process. During the early stages, keep the discussions moving. Try not to do too many things at once. Remember that during the planning, automation, or construction phases, the library must still function as a library. Books will still circulate, people will keep asking questions, and the phone will continue to ring. Plan for change carefully. Implement change deliberately.

The largest single item in your planning budget will be time. Planning committee meetings, an inventory of the community and the library, discussions, drafting the mission statement, selecting roles, objectives and goals will all take time. Budget time for both the staff and the director to work on planning. If the children's librarian is going to conduct a patron survey, suspend story hour until the survey is done. If the director is expected to be at both planning committee meetings and board of trustees meetings, consider cutting back on trustee meetings until the planning process is complete.

A modest sum of money should be allocated for printing and mailing costs. Another budget item to consider is refreshments for the planning committee. Food and light beverages can work wonders when meetings threaten to become tedious or bogged down in a dispute.

To summarize, when setting out to make a long range plan, the director and the planning committee would do well to follow the example of this piece of childhood doggerel:

> As you go through life,
> what ever may be your goal,
> Keep your eye upon the donut,
> And not upon the hole.

FIGURE 1-3: Danville Public Library Planning Budgets

MONEY

Item	Amount
Refreshments	$200.00
Publications/Photocopies	50.00
Printing and mailing	50.00
Total projected monetary budget	$300.00

People's time

Joan Myers, the Board of Trustees' representative on the planning committee will be excused from the monthly trustees' meeting. The Chair of the Board will keep her informed of issues before the Board and will vote her proxy.

The Assistant Librarian (who covers the reference desk) will help inventory in May. During this time, reference services will not be available until after 12 noon.

The Library Director is responsible for opening the library on Wednesday mornings. Since he is acting as the secretary to the planning committee, for the duration of this project, the library opening on Wednesdays will be delayed from 9:00 to 10:00, so that he can make a dent in the paperwork.

SUGGESTED READINGS

Peter Drucker's *Management: Tasks, Responsibilities, Practices* (Harper & Row, 1973) is a classic treatment of modern management practices. The section "Performance in the Service Institution" (Chapters 11 through 14) is especially important to those charged with managing a public library.

The Knowledge Institutions in the Information Age, (The Center for the Book, Library of Congress, 1988. The Center for the Book viewpoint series; no. 21.) an essay by R. Kathleen Molz is an inspired, thoughtful examination of the importance of public libraries in an era of instant information and communications. (Available from The Center for the Book, Library of Congress, Washington, DC 20540 (202) 707-5221.)

REFERENCES

1. Hobon, Burton. *Stamp Collecting As a Hobby*. New York, Sterling Publishing, 1986, pg. 117.

DIRECTIONS FOR WORKSHEETS

Worksheet 1-1
The library director and the trustees should draft a preliminary timetable before contacting people to sit on the planning committee. One of the first things prospective members will want to know is how much time they will have to commit. A timetable is a way to demonstrate that you are serious about planning.

Worksheet 1-2
The trustees and the director should also agree on the planning budgets.

WORKSHEET 1-1: Planning Committee Timetable

Planning Stage	Mo 1	Mo 2	Mo 3	Mo 4	Mo 5	Mo 6	Mo 7	Mo 8	Mo 9	Mo 10	Mo 11	Mo 12	Mo 13
Recruit Planning Committee													
1 st Committee Meeting													
Taking Inventory													
Draft Mission Statement													
Select Roles Formula Goals & Objectives													
Action Plan & Review													
Write & Distribute													

Notes:

_____

_____

_____

_____

_____

_____

_____

_____

_____

_____

WORKSHEET 1-2: Planning Budgets Worksheet

MONEY

Item	Amount

TOTAL PROJECTED MONETARY BUDGET

List below who will be working on the plan, and approximately how much time they will spend on planning.

2 THE PLANNING COMMITTEE

In one sense, every member of the community is a member of the planning committee. Everyone's expectations of what the library should represent to the community ought to be considered and weighed and fitted into the plan for the library's future. Clearly, dealing with the town's entire population as a committee is an impossibility. Your planning committee is, therefore, a representative body.

Who then should be represented on the planning committee? Both the people who will be doing the work (the library director and the board of trustees) and those whose needs you hope to meet (members of the community) should be represented by individual members on the planning committee.

Without exception, the library director should be a member of the planning committee. If the library is to become what the planning committee calls for it to become, then it must transform in the daily details. The plan must be sustained both day-to-day and year-to-year. The director, in charge of the day-to-day operations, must lead the library towards achieving the plan. To do this, the director must have an unshakable belief in the plan. The director is also an expert on the nuts and bolts of running a library. The committee will need this expertise to make sense of the technical aspects of what makes a library run.

Another essential element that will be needed for the library to successfully carry out the plan is the whole-hearted support of the board of trustees. A trustee should serve on the planning committee. Ideally, the trustee's representative would attend both the planning committee and board meetings. Given the amount of time this requires, it may not be possible to sit in on all those meetings. Make alternative arrangements to keep the trustee's rep informed of the board's doings, and the board informed of the planning committee's progress. Arrange for the rep to vote by proxy. Agendas, memos, minutes, phone calls, and faxes should be exchanged liberally between the two groups.

Under some circumstances, the entire board of trustees may want to be on the planning committee. While this may seem a comfortable solution—everybody already knows one other, everyone knows what the problems are, and so on—you run the risk of cutting the library off from "outsiders." Outsiders often have the advantage of coming to the situation fresh; they will have a different point of view. At the very least, they will be an outside confirmation that your original assumptions are correct. In addition, by reaching outside the library circle, you can expand the base of library supporters.

Ideally, a planning committee should have five members. An odd number of members ensures that votes will not come out to a tie, and it is easier to get five people together for a meeting than it is to get seven.

In selecting individuals to ask to be members of the planning committee, look for people who represent a particular constituency, while at the same time, can inquire after the needs and interests of other groups. They may not necessarily be current library users, but they must have at least some interest in the library, the community, books, and learning. Look for people who:

- play fair, have an open mind, and a feel for the common good;

- may not have been involved with the library before and may offer fresh insight;

- understand both the importance of details and a broad and far ranging perspective.

At this point in the planning process, two members of the committee can easily be named—the library director and the trustee's representative. To find others for the committee, these two should put their heads together, identify people that they would like to work with, and then contact the candidates.

DANVILLE'S PLANNING COMMITTEE

In addition to the library director and a trustee, DPL's committee came to include the recently retired high school physics teacher, a small business owner, and the supervisor of the first shift at the Danville Cordage Factory, who is also the parent of two junior high school students.

HOW TO ASK SOMEONE TO BE ON THE PLANNING COMMITTEE

When introducing the topic, explain why the library is creating a long range plan. Make it clear that you are asking them to be on the committee. The candidate will want to know what kind of commitment the committee will require. How often will we meet? When will our work be done by? Why are you asking me? Don't ask for an immediate answer. Give the candidate time to think it over. Follow up your offer with a letter and keep track of the process.

If you are turned down, ask if the candidate knows of anyone who might be interested in being on the committee. Thank the candidate for his time and consideration, and tell him that you will keep him posted on the library's work. (Just because someone turns you down doesn't mean that they aren't interested in the library. These are folks that you will want to send copies of the final plan to—potential library supporters. Again, follow up with a letter.)

FIGURE 2-1:

March 4

Mr. John Showalter
11 Bonair Drive
Danville

Dear John,

Good to run into you the other day. Retirement seems to be agreeing with you.

As I mention, the library is about to start putting together a long range plan. With the recent budget cuts, the trustees and I feel that we need to fall back, regroup and take a fresh look at the library's priorities.

Joan Myers (who has been a library trustee for several years now) is to head up the planning committee. She and I are currently out tapping folks to join us on the planning committee. Both Joan and I hope that you can join us on the committee; your insight into the community and the school system would be a most welcomed perspective.

At this point, we anticipate that the planning committee will issue its final report in March of next year. We expect that the committee will meet twice a month. Our first meeting is scheduled for April 3rd at 6:30 at the library.

John, I hope that you can join us. Please call if you have any questions. I'll give you a buzz next week.

Regards,

Philip Tullberg
Library Director

FIGURE 2-2:

March 23

Ms. Ruth Cohen, M.D.
Medical Arts Building
53 Winston Blvd.
Danville

Dear Ruth,

I was disappointed to hear that you are unable to sit on the library's long range planning committee. Both Philip and I will miss the wit and outlook that you would have brought to our undertaking, but we certainly understand the constraints on your time.

Knowing of your interest in the library, I'll be sure to send you a copy of the planning committee's report next March. In the meantime, should any ideas concerning the library occur to you, please give me a shout!

Best regards,

FIGURE 2-3: **Planning Committee Candidates**

Danville Public Library
Planning Committee Candidates

Person Contacted Name/Address/Phone	Outcome
John Showalter 11 Bonair Drive Danville 876-1874 (h)	Philip spoke w/, sent letter 3/4 Follow-up phone call 3/10, accepted
Dr. Joan Cohen 53 Winston Blvd. Danville 876-1532 (w)	Joan spoke w/ declined 3/20, letter sent Medical Arts Building 3/23
Elizabeth Yeats 128 Beacon Ave Danville 876-3413 (h)	Philip spoke w/, sent letter 3/1 Follow-up call 3/7. declined suggested Ann Nevill (876-2487)
William Blackwood 31 State Street Danville 873-1500	Joan wrote 3/3. Follow up call 3/7 declined
Ann Neville 49 Chester Street Danville 876-2487	Philip spoke w/ 3/9, accepted
Karen Repoza 21 Poplar Street Danville 876-1866	Joan spoke w/, follow-up letter 3/10 called 3/17, accepted

EVERY COMMITTEE NEEDS A CHAIR

The chair's first function is to ask questions, to start the discussion. What are we about? Who do we serve? What should we be doing? The chair's second job is to keep the discussion moving. A written agenda is very helpful. The chair may either be appointed by the board of trustees or the planning committee may elect its own officers.

HOW TO KEEP THE DISCUSSION MOVING

This may not be easy. Stick to deadlines (deadlines provide a sense of urgency). Take your cue from the group—if they look glassy eyed as someone goes on and on, get the discussion back on track, ask another question, ask someone else their opinion, or suggest a break for coffee.

The chair's third job is to see to it that the group reaches a consensus. Everyone on the committee may not agree on each and every item called for in the final plan (you may even still be listening to that same old argument from that same old so-and-so) but, by and large, everyone can live with the plan as a whole.

HOW TO HAVE BETTER MEETINGS

Start on time and don't let the meeting drag on: After about two and a half hours people's attention starts to wander. If you must meet past the two and a half hour mark, the chair should call a short break so that folks can get up and walk around for a minute. They will come back to the table refreshed.

Give people a chance to think things over: Some folks like to have the opportunity to "sleep on it," especially when it comes to important or complex issues. Don't follow every discussion with a vote.

Handle problems later: If the planning committee keeps going around and around on one particular issue, set it aside, come back to it later. If the issue continues to be contentious set it aside to be studied by a subcommittee. The subcommittee will make its recommendations to the entire committee at next months committee meeting.

Determine the specifics: As the planning committee moves through the planning process, it is tempting to settle all the details, dot all the "i's," and cross all the "t's," thereby setting exacting goals to be met to the last decimal place. The plan may spell things out in black and white, but it is not carved in stone. While some of the specifics may change, in terms of scope and direction, the plan outlines where the library intends to go. On our way there, however, we expect that we will have to make accommodations, and we may have to overcome some obstacles. Hopefully, no obstacle will be insurmountable.

Pick A Secretary: The committee needs a secretary. The secretary is responsible for keeping and distributing the minutes of the meetings, as well as preparing all the committee's paperwork. One of the most helpful things that the secretary can do, early in the planning process, is to distribute to the committee a list of the members' addresses and day and evening phone numbers. The secretary can also keep track of ideas as they emerge for the discussion. By using a large pad of paper and a marker to jot down key phases, the secretary can keep a running tally of ideas that come out of the committee's debates.

At the First Committee Meeting:

- Have the committee members introduce themselves.
- Review the planning timetable.
- Preview the planning process.
- Start taking inventory (Chapter 4).
- Set time for next meeting.
- Start to look at library statistics (Chapter 8).

DIRECTIONS FOR THE WORKSHEET

The library director and the trustees' rep should coordinate contacting candidates. It won't do for the trustee to ask Mr. Jones to join the committee just after he turned down the director.

Keep track of names and addresses. This information will become part of your library supporters database.

WORKSHEET 2-1: Planning Committee Candidates

Person Contacted:
Name/Address/Phone

Outcome

3 THE LIBRARY AND THE COMMUNITY

The community funds the library. Library users are members of the community. The library exists to serve the community. In turn, then the fate of the library is inexorably linked to the community. Our communities currently face the shifting demographics of an aging population, the proliferation of non traditional family structures, dramatic economic changes, and startling advances in technologies. For a library to survive, it must change as the community around it changes. A library must fit its community. It must respond to and anticipate the members of the community's needs for entertainment, enlightenment, and education. Libraries that fail to fit their communities, that fail to change as their community changes, run the risk of becoming moribund, irrelevant institutions.

FINDING THE FIT

Abraham Maslow (1908-1970) developed a theory of human motivation. He held that we have a hierarchy of needs. At the base of the hierarchy are our basic, physiological needs for food and water. Once we are fed and our thirst slaked, our next need is for safety, i.e., protection from attack and the elements. After we are safe and warm, then we seek love. Once we are loved, we begin to garner self-esteem, and only then can we start to become self-actualizing individuals.[1] Maslow's theory makes sense. Someone who is starving seeks food, not hugs and kisses. Walking down a poorly lit street in the shady part of town on a cold, rainy night, what I want most is to be home, drying my feet in front of the fire. Once I am home, and my beloved has brought me a soothing cup of tea, then I will be interested in being uplifted by the music of Mozart. But while I am walking down that mean street, the music of Mozart holds little allure.

Applying Maslow's theory to a community, we find that a town in the grips of a famine will have little interest in mounting an exhibit of the works of Cezanne. The funds for an arson investigation will be more readily available then funding for the public library, especially if the library is perceived to be in the same category as Mozart and Cezanne.

It is only by taking a broader view that we can see how the library can be considered on a par with public safety. If you are to have arson investigators, fire fighters, police officers, farmers, ranchers, and food distributors you must have education and information available. Education takes time. Transforming information into invention takes time. To be effective, the library must make its case before fire or famine breaks out. The library must anticipate the needs in its community. To do this, the library must understand what is going on outside its own four walls. From this understanding we must extrapolate and intuit where the community is going, what the community is becoming, what it will need in both the short and long term future, and how the library can help.

What are the long term trends in your community? Is your town gaining or losing population? Does the increase in population represent middle class flight from the crime ridden inner city, or the migration of folks whose first language isn't English, attracted by the jobs at the factory? How is your town changing?

And what of Mozart and Cezanne? Are they to vanish from the library, replaced by police sergeant examination study guides and adult reading primers? The ultimate aim of the library is to help users to get to Mozart and Cezanne—to find meaning, to think and understand the world around them, to see beyond their own experience, to catch a glimpse of the world as it spins. The police exam study guides and reading primers get them into the library, Cezanne and Mozart are the reasons for them to keep coming back.

When talking about community, consider the parable of the blind men and the elephant. Far from the gates of the city three blind men encountered an elephant. One grabbed the trunk and said "It is long and slender like a serpent." Another, feeling the ear said that it was rough and flat, like a leaf. The third, finding the leg, declared that it was large and round like a tree. Each man held onto his part of the elephant and the air was filled with the sounds of their words. Finally, after many hours, they agreed that this must be a wondrous beast with many parts. Working together, they climbed onto the back of the elephant and rode in triumph through the streets of the city.

The community is like the elephant. To a member of one of the founding families, the town is what was once Uncle Jack's farm and the school is where grandmother met grandfather. To the newcomer, downtown is a maze of one way streets. The library may find itself trying to serve the needs of a community increasingly at odds trying to define itself demographically, ethnically, culturally, and linguistically. In order to ride the elephant, a community must embrace its heritage, celebrate its diversity, and offer opportunity to all. For the library, this is more than an academic debate on multiculturalism or the changes wrought by an aging population. It has a very real impact on the services and materials that our users need.

Our users, our customers, live out there in the community. When they leave the library they go back out into that community. If we are to bring new customers into the library, we must reach out into that community. If we are to understand our customers' needs, we must try to see the world from their point of view.

The library must extend itself to two distinct groups within the larger community—those that currently use the library and those that do not. The point of reaching out to both groups is to:

1. gather information, impressions, and suggestions;

2. disseminate information about the library; and

3. establish and maintain goodwill.

GOODWILL DEFINED

Looking at a company's balancesheet, you may come across "goodwill" as a line item. According to *Munn's Encyclopedia of Banking and Finance* (an outstanding reference source) goodwill is intangible. It is completely non-physical. "It can never exist . . . but is established as a result of prestige gained over a period of years." The library must constantly and consistently seek the goodwill of the community that supports it.

Involve the community in the planning process. This is done by having people from the community on the planning committee. It is also done through the inventory stage of the planning process (this is covered in Chapter 4). There are many mechanisms to getting people into and involved in the library, but the key to genuine and successful community involvement is to have everyone associated with the library—the director, the trustees, staff, volunteers, and members of the Friends of the Library—tuned into people and willing to accommodate and change.

Now asking people for their input can be risky business. Once folks make suggestions and offer up ideas, they are quick to notice what becomes of their ideas. Be prepared to reply. If the library isn't going to act on some off the wall notion, politely thank the person, reiterate how important users' suggestions are, but that, for whatever reason, it is not possible to implement their idea.

WHAT'S WRONG WITH THIS SIGN?

The Foreign Language Collection Has Been Moved
To Its New Permanent Home on The Third Floor.
Ask a Librarian for Assistance!

For some users, going to the library is a tentative venture. Because of language, culture, lack of education, or economic status, some people may not know that the public library is free and open to all, or that the library has something for them. They may not feel entitled to use the library. For some, just walking into the large, imposing library building may be an act of courage. Once we get them into the library (a difficult enough task), we have to make them welcome. We have to keep them coming back, because these are the folks who need the library the most. For upwardly mobile, well-read types who love libraries, nothing is going to stop them from getting books, and you can be sure that if they don't find what they want, they're going to go and ask the librarian for assistance. Not everyone has the same sense of entitlement.

What's wrong with the sign? Imagine the frustration of the Vietnamese busboy who is told by a friend, "Oh yes. The library has books in Vietnamese. Just go in and go up one flight of stairs, and they are on the right." He walks into the strange building, goes up the stairs, takes a right, and finds a wide selection of magazines in English. Will he steel himself and ask for help? If he doesn't, if he flees the building, how long will it be before he comes into the library again? If only the sign had been in Vietnamese.

To successfully serve the community we must try to see through our users' eyes. You may think that you are effectively communicating your message, but are you communicating in a way that your intended recipient can understand? Posters announcing a literacy program are not nearly as effective as announcements on the radio. Signs in English pointing the way to the foreign language collection send the wrong message.

The library serves the community one individual at a time. Each reference question, each circulation transaction, every time someone comes through our door, represents an opportunity for the library to fulfill its promise.

CIVIC CELEBRATIONS

Old Home Days. The Harvest Festival. Fourth of July. Pioneer Days. Founders Day. First Night. Most towns have at least one communal, annual civic celebration. We may fire the cannon on the town common, show the fruits of our harvest, ride down main street on horseback, or read the Declaration of Independence from the steps of town hall. These events can be seen as symbolic gestures. They provide insight into what the town values. They are symbols of what the people who live here consider important—liberty, adventurousness, hard work, determination. Is there some way that the public library can reflect these values? Can the library tap into the same wellspring that nourishes these celebrations? Could the library become an embodiment of these values? At the least, the library should participate in these events. Hold the book sale on the Fourth of July, have an open house on First Night. Eventually, looking at the town's celebrations, the monuments and historic sites, how the streets are laid out and who they are named for, where the big, expensive houses are and where the not so big houses are, you may catch a glimpse of what makes the town tick. Once you know that, then you will know what kind of library the town should have.

SUGGESTED READINGS

Sontag, Deborah "New Immigrants Test Nation's Heartland." *New York Times*, October 18, 1993. Pg. 1+.

Hoffert, Barbara. "¡Se Lea Español Aqu!" *Library Journal*, July 1992. Pg. 34-37.

REFERENCES

1. *The New Encyclopedia Britannica* 15th edition. Chicago: University of Chicago Press, 1987. Micropeadia, vol. 7. Pg. 911.

TAKING INVENTORY

At its simplest, the planning process takes what you have—your building, staff and trustees, collections and community—and uses them to get what you need: a larger building, a new computer, more staff. Using the worksheets in the last half of this chapter, you can start to take stock.

When you make an inventory, identify what you currently have on hand in your library and your town. Taking inventory is an opportunity to get out and take the measure of your community. Check your assumptions about who you serve and what they want. Here is where you look in greater detail at the mission question, "Who is our customer?" Who are the library users, and the non-users, in your community?

Some of the items that you enumerate in the inventory may be of immediate importance to your library. Consider the following example scenarios before embarking on taking inventory:

Example A: The county is currently building a retirement home and senior center three blocks from your library. The facility will house one hundred and fifty residents, as well has offer programs and services to non-resident seniors. This event may cause a significant shift in your user population and the services that they require. By offering services specifically to this constituency, you may find that you have a group of older friends, supporters, volunteers, and bene-factors.

On the other hand, some of what you find may not be useful right away. But later, when you are in the middle of putting your plan into action, you may reach into this bag of tricks and pull out a gold nugget that you didn't even know that you had.

Example B: You run into one of the lawyers that you identified while taking inventory. You mentioned that the library just received the latest edition of the Martindale-Hubble legal directory. She didn't know that the library had that—now she doesn't have to buy it! She is *very* pleased. She starts to use the library's reference section every so often. Two years later, she offers to shepherd your plans for the library addition through the State Historical Commission's approval process.

Most of us grow use to our surroundings rather quickly. In a new town we notice every gas stations, hardware store, and bakery. But at home, we tend to take the scenery for granted.

Example C: When the new mall opened last year there were balloons and fireworks. After the first couple of visits, though, it becomes a part of our every day world. We forget how life was before the mall. We forget to remember that things have changed because of the mall. Yet, for our town, things have changed. Merchants may have moved from Main Street to the mall. Kids may now "hang" at the mall and not at the park. More people may drive down Oak Street, past the library, on their way to the mall.

To Do: Try to see your town for the first time. Walk down your town's main street, and pretend that you are new in town. What do you see? Drive out to the mall, or the three-year-old sub-division. Walk through the park or along the lake. Is it as you remember it? What has changed?

Ask yourself: If you were new in town, how would you find the library? Are there signs in the center of town pointing the way? Have the hedges overgrown the lettering on the side of the building that spells out "Public Library?"

To Do: Skim through the yellow pages of the local phone book. What businesses use the library? Who might be interested in your services?

An inventory provides a snapshot of your community and your library. It will serve as the starting point for comparison as you meet your current plan's objectives, and it will help the next planning committee, five to eight years down the road, to understand why you did what you did.

Example D: When you are conducting your inventory it is important not to avoid the unpleasant or the unpopular. The proposed closing of the local Army base means saving millions of Federal dollars, but it also means the loss of thousands of local jobs. The library is buying more books and videos on interviewing and resume writing. A professor from the State University's business program recently spoke at the library on starting your own business, and the county agent gave a demonstration of home canning methods.

Libraries are, of course, better at serving the needs of its users than in serving the needs of its non-users. As part of your inventory determine who your non-users are. This may require some imagination on your part. Canvass a neighborhood on a warm, spring Saturday afternoon. Stop people as they walk through the mall. Ask if they use the library? Do they know where it is? Distribute handouts that describe the library's hours, location, a little bit about the collection and services, and information on how to get a library card.

DANVILLE'S UNSERVED POPULATION

The director of the Danville library, while browsing through the registered borrowers noticed that very few borrowers were from the west side of the Danville River. Other neighborhoods, some even further from the library then West Side, were well represented. The row houses of West Side had originally been built to house factory workers and their families. As soon as they gained a leg up the economic ladder, people left West Side from some of the more comfortable neighborhoods. For many of the current residents of West Side, English is not their primary language.

Some of the numbers that you gather in your inventory will be important when you start to Keep Score, later in the planning process.

To determine Circulation per Capita (the first of the statistics in Chapter 8), you will need to know how many people live in your community and how many books are borrowed from your library, both numbers you find during the inventory. Then, by dividing your circulation by your population, you have Circulation per Capita.

Later, once you are comfortable with your statistics, you'll be able to refine what you measure. When you know how many people attend programs at the library, then you may be interested in how many pre-teens attend library programs. Is this a growing segment of your user population? Is this a group that you could better serve with programmed events at the library?

STATISTICAL SOURCES

Many communities have a planning or development agency. It may be at the municipal or county level, or certainly there is someone at the state level. These folks can tell you how many kids between five and 13 live in your town, how many single-parent households there are, and if in five years time there will be a need for a new high school or senior center.

If you don't know where to start looking for demographic data and projections, call your state library. Someone in the reference or government document section will help you start to locate sources.

ANECDOTAL EVIDENCE

While there is no substitute for cold figures and hard facts, personal stories can be far more compelling. It is one thing to say that 35 percent of the town's business owners regularly use the library. But when a business owner talks about how a book that he borrowed help him to spot an emerging trend that was a boon to his ailing enterprise, it is far more dramatic and memorable. The business owner's testimony helps put a face on the number. Sure, 35 percent use the library, but here is an actual person talking about how the library made a difference to him.

Ask your users for their stories. When someone comes up to you at the gas station to tell you how the library really helped them to tackle a tough problem, ask them if they would mind putting it in writing. Make up story forms that ask people to describe how the library has made a difference to them (see Figures 4-1 and 4-2). Put a stack of them out on the circulation desk. Keep collecting this anecdotal evidence. Have everyone associated with the library (staff, trustees, friends, and relatives) alert for library success stories.

Besides creating powerful arguments for the library, these stories help your users to remember just how important the library is to them. It may make it easier for them to be advocates for the library when it comes time to vote for funding.

OTHER THINGS TO DO

Write up a story form for your library. Have a stack of them out on the reference and circulation desks.

Ask yourself who doesn't use the library? Why don't they use the library? Investigate.

DIRECTIONS FOR WORKSHEETS

Worksheet 4-1
All the members of the planning committee, the board of trustees and the library staff should walk around town, pretending that they are newcomers. The planning committee should collect and consider these impressions.

Worksheets 4-2 and 4-3
The community and library profile worksheets will help you to get started in taking your inventory. Remember, every town and every library is different, so add your own items to those that we have listed here. If your community or library doesn't have something listed on the worksheets, compare and contrast. Why doesn't your town have a recreation department? Does it have something else instead?

FIGURE 4-1: **Tell Us About It!**

The Danville Public Library is dedicated to the education and enlightenment of all the people of this community.

We are here to serve you!

Tell us why you use the library! How has the library helped you? Let us know what you think about your library!

Place the completed form in the suggestion box in the library's vestibule or mail to Librarian, Danville Public Library, 12 Elm Street, Danville, USA.

Optional information

Name:

Address:

Phone number:

FIGURE 4-2: Another Example of a Story Form

Speak out for America's Libraries

Libraries Change Lives

I believe America's libraries play a vital role in empowering people of all ages to learn and grow and to exercise their right to know in a democratic society. I believe our nation's libraries must be fully supported in the Information Age.

Help celebrate America's Libraries. Tell us in 100 words or less how the library and/or librarian helped to change your life or made a difference for you or someone you know. Your "success story" will be used to support the case for library funding with legislators and policymakers at the local, state and national levels and to tell others how the library can help.

Who knows? It could change someone's life.

Your library "success story"/comments (please type or print):

_____

_____

_____

_____

_____

You have permission to quote me for publicity purposes.

_____   _____
Signature   Date

_____
Your name (please print)   Address   City, State   ZIP

_____
Parent's signature (if under 18)

Return this statement to your local library, or fold, stamp and send to: **Rally for America's Libraries**
American Library Association
50 E. Huron St.
Chicago, IL 60611

WORKSHEET 4-1: First Impressions (Again)

Overtime we all become accustomed to our surroundings. When we first come to a new town, we notice every gas station, school, and hardware store, but, once we have passed through a couple of times, these details blend into the woodwork.

Walk around town or your neighborhood. Ask yourself what's new, what's difference, what's changing?

Please record your impressions and then pass them along to a member of the planning committee.

_____

_____

_____

_____

_____

_____

_____

_____

_____

_____

_____

_____

_____

_____

WORKSHEET 4-2: Community Profile

Your Town:

Date:

How many people live in the community (or communities) that you serve?

Approximately how many members of your community are:

less than 5 years old?

between 5 & 13?

14 & 18?

19 & 65?

over 65?

What languages are spoken by the people who live in your town?

How many single-parent households are there?

List the professionals in your community:

- Doctors

(continued)

WORKSHEET 4-2:   (Cont.)

- Lawyers

- Accountants

- Bankers

- Business Owners

- Real Estate Developers

- Other Big Wheels

Who is your town's largest employer? What do they make? How many people do they employ? Do they have an in-house library?

Who else employs many of the people who live in your community?

Are there any other significant businesses or industries in your area?

Roughly what percentage of your community is unemployed?

Are there many home-based businesses in your town?

Is your town a seasonal community?

What newspapers cover local news?

List the local radio stations, book stores, video outlets, and record stores.

WORKSHEET 4-2:   (Cont.)

Does your town have a community access cable channel?

List the schools in your town—Are they local or regional? Public or private?

- Elementary

- Secondary

- High

- Vocational/ Technical

- Colleges/Universities

Are there many home schoolers in your town?

List the medical care organizations in your community—

- Hospitals

- Clinics

- Long term and rehabilitation facilities

- Hospices

List the social service providers in your community—What programs do they offer?

- Nursing Homes

- Day Care Centers

WORKSHEET 4-2: (Cont.)

- Shelters/Halfway Houses/Drug Treatment Centers

- Youth & Recreation Centers

List the service organizations in your town -

- Historical Society

- Boy/Girls Club, Scouts, etc.

- Rotary/Lions/Moose, etc.

- Churches

Is your town a county seat?

Are there any state or county offices in your town?

What form of government governs your town?

Does your town have a long-range or capital improvement plan?

WORKSHEET 4-3: Library Profile

Your Library:

Date:

How many people are registered at the library? How many are residents? How many are non-residents?

How many books (or titles) are in your library?

How many items were checked out of your library last year?

How many reference questions were you asked last year?

How many hours do volunteers work in your library?

How are capital improvements funded at your library?

What are the sources of your operating income?

- Trust Funds

- Friends Group

- Town Appropriation

- Other

(continued)

WORKSHEET 4-3:   (Cont.)

What facilities do you offer your patrons?

- Photocopier

- Fax

- Meeting rooms

- Other

Do you have a computer?

Do you use an on-line services for:

- Inter-library loan

- Accessing an electronic mail service

- Reference/research

Do you charge patrons directly for on-line searching?

Do you have any reference cd's?

How are your trustees selected?

5 MISSION

> . . . And Crispin Crispian shall ne'er go by
> From this day to the ending of the world,
> But we in it shall be remembered;
> We few, we happy few, we band of brothers;
> For he to-day that sheds his blood with me
> Shall be my brother; be he ne'er so vile,
> This day shall gentle his condition:
> And gentlemen in England a-bed
> Shall think themselves accursed they were not here,
> And hold their manhoods cheap whiles any speaks
> That fought with us upon Saint Crispin's day.
>
> —*King Henry V*, Act IV, Scene III

After giving this speech, if we are to believe Shakespeare, the young King Henry, marching on Calais, led his troops against the far larger French army. On October 25th, the feast day of Saints Crispin and Crispian, in 1414, in the woods known as Agincourt, Henry and his men prevailed. Calais fell in October. By mid November, King Henry was back in London where crowds lined the streets and hailed the hero of Agincourt. For King Henry, and those that marched with him, the conquest of France was another step toward their ultimate goal: Jerusalem. For them, the battle at Agincourt was part of a Crusade.[1] Henry V was a seasoned leader who believed fervently in his cause. His skills, his passionate belief in what he was doing, his very being, inspired his soldiers to victory against what seemed to be overwhelming opposition. The English won on Saints Crispin and Crispian's Day because they believed in their leader and their mission.

Although it may not seem so at times, leading a library is far easier, and safer, than leading a Crusade (more than 7,000 men fell at Agincourt). The sense of battling overwhelming odds, however, seems familiar. Yet, a belief in a mission and the ability to see the small, everyday occurrences that get things done in terms of that overarching purpose has allowed not only medieval armies to prevail, but also modern organizations.

A mission statement answers the question, "What is our purpose?", in the broadest possible terms. A sweeping, idealistic understanding of purpose can guide an organization through times of radical changes in technologies and social practices.

Consider the changes brought about because of the invention and mass production of automobiles. Most of the people who made buggy whips went out of business—but not all. Some companies that produced equestrian-related products survived and prospered after the advent of the car. "Body by Fisher" appeared for years on the frames of cars built by General Motors. Fisher Body Company started as a horse drawn carriage maker. If they had seen their purpose to be makers of horse drawn carriages, most likely they would have gone out of business, like all the other horse drawn carriage makers. But by seeing themselves as being in the transportation business they could adopt to a change in technology, shift from carriages to auto bodies, and eventually become a major division of a large and important transportation concern. Hermes was founded as a maker of saddle blankets. While they made very nice saddle blankets, they were just saddle blankets none the less. When most people no longer required saddles, the demand for saddle blankets dropped dramatically. Hermes did not define itself as a saddle blanket maker, rather, they were in the business of providing fine goods to the carriage trade. They do this to this day, selling scarfs and neckties at prices that stagger the imagination.

While public libraries may, for some, conjure up images of the horse and buggy era, there will always be a need for the library's basic business. There will always be a need for information.

THE NATURE OF THE MISSION

With a clear, unwavering sense of a mission, it is easier for an organization to focus its resources on attaining its purpose. Frances Hesselbein, former executive director of the Girl Scouts of America (GSA), calls this managing for mission. In 1976, when Hesselbein became the head of the Girl Scouts, it was in danger of foundering. Offering merit badges for "Good Grooming" and "Hosting a Party," the GSA was increasingly irrelevant in a society that was faced with rising teenage pregnancy, drug use, child abuse, and homelessness. Membership had been dropping for close to a decade. With more women starting to work fulltime outside the home, the GSA was having trouble recruiting troop leaders. The Boy Scouts were studying the possibility of allowing girls to join their group. In turning the Girl Scouts around, Hesselbein started with its mission. She asked, "what is our business? "and" who are our customers?" The Scouts' basic purpose has always been to help girls achieve their highest potential. What had changed was the customer, and what she wanted. In the late 1970's, teenaged girls were more interested in computers, the environment, and business than they were in cooking, sewing, and housekeeping. Scouting had always been associated with white, middle class, suburban communities. Under Hesselbein, the GSA fostered a policy of opening the doors of scouting to all girls, developing scouting programs in low income and minority neighborhoods, rewriting the Girl Scout handbook to include a more diverse outlook, and recruiting troop leaders who were role models. By 1990, membership had grown to 2.3 million girls, 15% of whom were from minority groups, and the two most popular merit badges were "Math Wiz" and "Computer Fun."[2] While much may have changed about the Girl Scouts, the mission has remained the same.

THE UNIVERSAL TRUTH

Missions don't change over time. A mission is based on some universal truth or need. The need for transportation, the desire for luxury goods, the necessity of helping children realize their potential will always be with us. These mission truths can be found in the Latin motto on a coat-of-arms, in the words of the institution's founders, or etched in stone on the face of the building. By themselves, these words may sound faintly ridiculous. Neglect it over time, and this truth can become a mocking remnant of a romantic past. By integrating the missionary truth into a mission statement, the truth becomes a springboard towards its own realization.

A mission statement allows an organization to share a common vision—a common understanding of purpose and direction. A mission statement is made up of three parts: the library's truth, and the answers to two questions, "What is our business?" and "Who are our customers?" Our business and our customers may change over time, but the truth will remain the same. Later in the planning process you will have a chance to examine in greater detail who your customers are and what your business is. For the mission statement, the answers to these mission questions should be general. Our customers are the people of Danville. Our business is to provide library services.

A quick look at the history of American public libraries shows a progression of purpose and suggests some universal truths. In the 1700s, social libraries were formed by individuals who associated for the purpose of enlightened discussion and mutual inquiry. Circulating libraries, also an eighteenth century institution, were founded as commercial ventures that lent books to borrowers for a fee. The owners of circulating libraries were not interested in cultural exchange, improving the minds of their users, or improving the education of the community. Their goal was to make a profit on their investment. This economic imperative meant the circulating libraries carried popular, not scholarly, titles. Gentlemen and scholars borrowed books and attended meetings at the social library. The latest novels were to be found at the circulating library. Public libraries as we now know them, grew out of the nineteenth century movement toward universal public education. To the founders of this period, the missions of the library " . . . were specific and very real. They wished to promote equality of educational opportunity, to advance scientific investigation, to save the youth from the evils of an ill-spent leisure, and to promote the vocational advance of the workers. In short, they were . . . interested in normative ends—in the improvement of men and women and through them of society."[3]

DEFINING YOUR MISSION

To begin the search for your library's mission, look to the past. Study the founding of the library. What motivated the civic leaders of that time to start a public library? What were the library's early benefactors hoping to accomplish with their gifts? At the heart of the library's history lie universal truths: children should be educated, a democracy requires a literate citizenry, and educated men and women lead more productive lives. Although much has changed, this central truth is as valid today as it was when the library was founded.

When defining your mission look for high concept words, phrases in Latin, high brow words, words that are so earnest that they almost make you blush (see Figure 5-1). If, after scouring the historic record, the planning committee can't find words that inspire a sense of mission, then it is up to the present committee to put down on paper the library's missionary truth.

The universal truth is the cornerstone of a successful library. All the library's objectives and activities must be evaluated in light of the universal truth. Does this activity bring us closer to our truth? How will it bring us closer to fulfilling our mission?

SPECIFYING THE TRUTH

The library's truth should not be a secret. Everyone who works at the library—the director, staff, volunteers, the Friends who run the book sale—needs to know the central truth, and understand how

FIGURE 5-1: Words to Look for . . .

Dedicated	Enlightenment	History
Established	Education	Posterity
Founded	Industry	Children
Provide	Wisdom	Citizens
	Recreation	People
	Leisure	Adults
	Improvement	Future
	Truth	
	Beauty	

they contribute to that truth and the library's mission. This may sound "touchy feely," but values are reflected in the subtleties. Details such as the way the phone is answered, the dust covering the suggestion box, or even the wording of an overdue notice all say a lot about a library. We succeed only when our deeds line up with our purpose. Time should regularly be set aside so that everyone at the library can discuss the library's mission statement and how what they are doing furthers that mission.

THE MISSION QUESTIONS

A universal truth is an abstraction. For the truth to become real, we must be much more specific. The steps of the planning process move from the absolute idealism of the library's truth, to the reality of day to day activities. The next step on the road to reality is to ask the key mission questions, "What is our business?" and "Who is our customer?" These questions link our quest for a universal truth to what we are doing, and to the people that we are doing it for. By taking the library's universal truth and combining it with the answers to these key questions, a mission statement can be crafted. The library's mission statement is only slightly less abstract than the library's truth, but it is closer to reality.

THE TRUTH IN DANVILLE

While combing through the library's early history, the Planning Committee came across a modest bequest given to the library by one of its earliest users. The deed of gift required that the money was to be spent in such a way "so as to enrich the lives of others as it has done for me so often." Here then, was the universal truth for the Danville Public Library—to enrich lives. The Committee then asked itself, "What is our business?" and "Who is our customer?" It is the business of the library to provide materials and services and access those materials that contain recorded knowledge, experience, and wisdom. The library's customers were the people of Danville. From this, the Planning Committee drafted the following mission statement: "*The Danville Library offers materials and services which provide access to the recorded knowledge, experience, and wisdom of others to enrich the lives of all the members of our community.*"

THE PUBLIC LIBRARY'S MISSION

The public library is blessed in its mission. Look at the other municipal agencies. Given a choice, everyone would prefer not to use the police or fire department; the public works department, while necessary, disrupts our lives as it fixes the roads or repairs the water main; the schools and the recreation department cater to kids and teenagers. The library is for everyone. Going to the library is really a treat. There are all those books, videos, and cd's that you can take home! If you call up on the phone and ask a question, someone will try to find an answer for you. Since taxes pay for the library, borrowing a book, asking a reference question, or attending a program doesn't cost anything extra. To the user, the library is free. With all this in its favor, how can a library help but generate goodwill?

HOW TO DISCUSS AN ABSTRACTION

- Pose the question: What is the library's truth?
- Offer up background information.
- Seek to define your terms.
- Let people respond.

- Allow time for discussion, both at the meeting where the question is first posed, and then, also at the next committee meeting. Folks sometimes come up with great insights if they are allowed to cogitate awhile.

- Jot down key phases and ideas.

- Look for common themes.

- Put together an answer to your original question.

SUGGESTED READING/VIEWING

John Byrne's article "Profiting from the Nonprofits," (*Business Week*, March 26, 1990, pages 66-74) puts the lessons from the best run nonprofit organizations in a nutshell.

For a dramatic (and entertaining) demostration of a sense of mission, watch Kenneth Branagh's 1989 production of *Henry V.*

In 1989, Public Library Quarterly published a series on the mission statemens of different libraries from across the U.S. All the articles are titled "The Mission of the Public Library." The specific cites are:

- Vol. 9 (1) 1989, pp. 35-38,

- Vol. 9 (2) 1989, pp. 37-40,

- Vol. 9 (3) 1989, pp. 31-36,

- Vol 10 (1) 1990, pp. 23-24, and

- Vol. 10 (3) 1990, pp. 29-30.

REFERENCES

1. Ashley, Maurice. *Great Britain to 1688*. Ann Arbor, The University of Michigan Press, 1961. (The University of Michigan History of the Modern World) pp. 154-157.
2. Byrne, John. "Profiting from the Nonprofits." *Business Week* March 26, 1990, pp. 66-74.

3. Shera, Jesse H. *Foundations of the Public Library: the Origans of the Public Library Movement in New England 1629-1855.* The Shoe String Press, 1965, pp 247.

DIRECTIONS FOR WORKSHEETS

A member of the planning committee (or perhaps several members) should research the library's history. Go through the minutes of early trustee meetings, check with the historical society, and talk with people who may remember the library's founding or are related to an early benefactor. Prepare a short presentation to the full planning committee.

Worksheet 5-1
Use the "Looking for the Library's Truth" worksheet to start a discussion about your library's truth. See if you can find a truth. Allow about an hour for discussion. If an answer seems close at hand, continue; if not, break off the discussion. In any event, come back to the question at the next committee meeting.

Worksheet 5-2
As you near agreement on the library's truth, distribute the "Mission Questions" worksheet. Discuss and answer.

Take your library's truth and the answers to your mission questions and draft a mission statement.

WORKSHEET 5-1: Looking for the Library's Truth

What were the circumstances that lead to the founding of your library?

Has your library been the recipient of a bequest? Why was the bequest made? What did the deed of gift say? Examine each substantial gift that your library has received over the years.

Is your library named for someone? What attributes are associated with that person? Youthful vigor? Steadfast thrift? Relentless inquiry?

WORKSHEET 5-2: The Mission Questions

What is our business?

_____

_____

_____

_____

_____

_____

_____

Who are our customers?

_____

_____

_____

_____

_____

_____

_____

SELECTING ROLES

Mission statements express noble, lofty ideas. However, fulfilling your mission requires more specific action. Defining your library's roles is the first step in moving from the idealism of the mission statement to the concrete reality of day-to-day tasks. By breaking your mission down into small, "bite-sized" pieces, you will end up with To Do lists of activities, based on your mission statement, as well as free and frank discussions with members of your community.

To create a meaningful plan, you need to determine the primary and secondary role that your library plays in your community. These major roles will determine how you will spend your resources.

There is a hard truth that necessitates selecting two, and only two, major roles for your library. If you try to do everything for all of the people all of the time, you will fail to achieve your mission and you will be miserably confused to boot. There simply aren't enough hours in the day, dollars in the budget, or people on the staff for any library to hope to play any more than two roles in its community.

Consider what would happen in your library if, within the first twenty minutes of opening one morning, the kindergarten teacher came by to drop off a list of recommended easy readers, someone called wanting information on the Americans with Disabilities Act, the mail carrier delivered books and needed your signature, a patron wanted to renew a book that had a mile-long waiting list, and an Elk came in and asked if his group could use the library's meeting room next Saturday. All of these are legitimate requests for your time and attention. The only way to know what to do first, then second, then third, is to have a clear sense of what your priorities are. To select roles is to begin to set those priorities.

The New York Public Library (NYPL), holding more than 46 million items, has the second largest collection in the United States. With 3,000 employees and a budget of $132 million, the four non-lending research libraries and the eighty-two branch libraries serve the 2.9 million residents of the Bronx, Manhattan, and Staten Island. The NYPL has 1.4 million registered patrons. Each year the NYPL librarians answer more than 5 million reference questions while close to half a million people attend library programs.[1] Yet the NYPL has only two major roles.

1. The research libraries support scholars.

2. The branch libraries have targeted the city's children as their most important constituency.

The NYPL serves, literally, millions, yet they have selected two groups, kids and scholars, as their most important users.[2] This doesn't mean that they don't provide reference services, or copies of the hottest best sellers. It just means that services to children and scholars are the top priority.

So what are the roles that public libraries play? In 1987, the American Library Association identified seven roles that libraries fill in their communities (see Figure 6-1).

DEFINING YOUR LIBRARY'S ROLE

Elements of all these roles will be found, to a greater or lesser extent, in almost all public libraries. You must evaluate the PLA roles in the context of your library facilities and staff, and the community that you serve.

If your library is pressed for space, it will be more difficult to be a Center for Community Activity, then if you have just unveiled a new building. Likewise, if the people in your town use the high school stage for candidate night and the Grange Hall for concerts, there may not be a need for the library to be an activity center.

Try to build on your strengths. If someone on your staff has a flair for answering reference questions, consider selecting "Reference Library" as a major role. On the other hand, if your ace reference librarian is contemplating retirement, you will need to carefully examine that role. Roles change over time.

When the Avondale Branch Library and Resource Center (Birmingham, AL) saw that its circulation was falling, they reevaluated the library role in the community. Since the nearby high school had been converted to a middle school, they notice that most of their patrons were now school-aged kids. The library became a "homework library." With a Community Block Grant they renovated the library, added computers and educational software to the collection, and recruited adults to help young students with their homework.[3]

Most of the library's resources (time, people, and money) should be earmarked for your two major roles.

FIGURE 6-1: Public Library Roles

Community Activities Center: The library is a central focus point for community activities, meetings, and services.

Community Information Center: The library is a clearinghouse for current information on community organizations, issues, and services.

Formal Education Support Center: The library assists students of all ages in meeting educational objectives established during their formal courses of study.

Independent Learning Center: The library supports individuals of all ages pursuing a sustained program of learning independent of any educational provider.

Popular Materials Library: The library features current, high-demand, high-interest materials in a variety of formats for persons of all ages.

Preschoolers' Door to Learning: The library encourages young children to develop an interest in reading and learning through services for children, and for parents and children together.

Reference Library: The library actively provides timely, accurate, and useful information for community residents.

Research Center: The library assists scholars and researchers to conduct in-depth studies, investigate specific areas of knowledge, and create new knowledge.

When working with the ALA roles, you may want to expand and refine the definitions of your major roles. Your roles should be focused and meaningful within the context of your community.

ROLE EXAMPLES

The Tulsa City-County Library system (Tulsa, OK) saw that one of the major roles that it plays in its community is "Popular Materials Library." They interpreted this role to mean that the collection should feature "a wide variety of recreational reading for all ages, both fiction and nonfiction, in a variety of formats, which meets the standards set forth in the collection development policy. Subjects for purchase should include books of current interest, books about the arts and entertainment, classics, standard titles, fiction titles in all genres, how-to's, and other materials that would appeal to a broad range of readers."[4] Once they had specifically described what "Popular Material Library" meant to them, they created goals and objectives to make the role a reality. The collection was evaluated, subject areas were targeted for improvement, and the acquisition process was streamlined.

At the Richards Free Library (Newport, NH) the director and trustees noticed three disturbing trends. There was a high drop out rate at the regional high school, a slowdown in the local economy and industry was leaving the area. They realized that a literate and well-trained work force could be a key element in attracting new employers to their town. In response, the library has defined its primary role as a "Door to Learning," and seeks to encourage continuous self-education for all. Combining the ALA's "Independent Learning Center" and "Preschoolers Door to Learning" roles, the library offers specific programs and services to preschoolers, school aged children, adult new readers, and those seeking a greater understanding of contemporary ideas and issues.[5]

Finding your library's roles

- Look at the results of the inventory. Who uses your library? Who doesn't use your library? Why?

- "That's always been a problem...." If something has always been a problem, then, unless steps are taken to correct the situation, it will continue to be a problem. It is always possible that it will cease to be a problem on its own, but, by and large, the laws of inertia apply. Study the problem for different points of view. Encourage people to suggest ways to fix the problem. Be prepared to try a couple of different approaches before hitting on something that works.

- How is the community changing? How can the library help?
- What do people think the library *should* be?

HOW THE DPL DETERMINED ITS ROLES

STUDY SAYS THAT HALF OF ADULTS IN U.S. CAN'T READ OR HANDLE ARITHMETIC[6]

"Look at this," said the planning committee member who had just passed out copies of this newspaper headline and the attending article. "I find it appalling that half of the adults in this country can't look at a train schedule, and their watch, and then tell you when the next train is due! The other day I was in McDonald's for lunch. The woman in the next line was having trouble ordering. She wanted 10 chicken nuggets, but they only come in packages of nine or eleven. The clerk was getting exasperated and kept rolling his eyes up to the big sign that spells out the menu. 'It's all up there on the sign,' he kept saying. Why, it was a clear as day that this woman couldn't read. I was dumbfounded! All this talk about computers, and videos and multimedia is a lot of hogwash if going to McDonalds is a trial and an ordeal!" A spirited discussion followed. Are we going to be teaching people their abc's? What about folks who *can* read but don't? Can we help people to think beyond soundbites, helping them to develop insight into their world and their selves? Maybe we could help them to find out how to fix a lamp, or find a job, or raise a kid. What if someone is taking a night school class? How can we help people if they don't come into the library? Eventually, the planning committee agreed that, as its primary role, *the library is a center for independent and assisted learning.*

"Here we go again! Someone griping about the middle school kids . . . " said the director to himself as he read through the library's suggestion box. The Danville Library is two blocks from the middle school, and, it seemed that every afternoon, the kids congregate in the downstairs hallway and talk and carry on. The staff asks them to be quiet, but, twenty minutes later they're at it again. They're not bad kids, its just that they drift over to the library while they wait for the late bus, or for their folks to pick them up after work. They really bug some of the other patrons, and the staff hate keeping after them to keep it down to a dull roar. Looking into it, the DPL discovered that the middle school library was often used as a meeting space by after school organizations, and that, besides, it wasn't considered "cool" to hang out at school after hours. Those on the cutting edge of adolescent fashion tended to wander by the local convenience store, and then, once they had worn out their welcome, shifted over to the library. There wasn't really another place for them to be in the mid to late afternoon. What if the library turned the situation around and welcomed the kids? Set aside one of the meeting rooms as a place for study and quiet conversation, maybe provide help with homework? In this, the planning committee discovered the DPL's secondary role, *the library is a source of support for grade school students.*

It is tempting to try to fit everything that the library does into one, all encompassing role. When defining the library's roles, don't make them too broad. The mission statement can be expansive, ideal, and picturesque; selecting and defining the library's roles starts to give focus. Roles should be fairly precise and give direction to the library's activities.

As you get closer to selecting your major roles, you may notice, with a sense of growing uneasiness, the list of "leftover" roles. And these roles seem fairly important. Keep in mind that while a role may not be a major role at your library, you may still have to deal with some aspects of that role. Even if "Community Information Center" is in the pile of leftover roles, you must still provide some basic information about your town. You may not have the environmental impact statement filed by the developers of the proposed subdivision, but you know where your patron can go to get a copy.

In fact, you may choose to ignore a role all together, but you must be very deliberate in your ignorance and not be trying to wish a role away. Few small libraries are "Research Centers". Yet a library may house primary sources that would be of interest to someone doing genealogical research: old newspapers, telephone books, journals, letters and photographs. If no one has the time to catalog these moldy oldies, they are often relegated to the attic, and will literally go away when the wood pulp in the paper turns to dust. A more attractive alternative is for the library to declare that it is many things, but it is not a "Research Center," and, as such, it does not have the resources needed to properly house these relics, and then pass the collection on to the town's historical society.

With only limited amounts of the library's resources available for allocation among all its the leftover roles, it is important to form a well thought-out contingency plan for the roles that you don't select. If we're not a "Community Activities Center," where can the Elks meet? If we're a "Popular Materials Center," and a patron wants to do in depth research on an arcane topic, what will we do? *Leftover roles can often be effectively managed through one time or low maintenance projects*. This is where the administrative role comes in. For example, in-depth research needs could be managed by establishing an informal relationship with a library that is research oriented. The reference staff at the local college library may be happy to help your users (see Figure 6-2).

All libraries require a certain amount of administrative care and feeding. In addition to public service roles that need to be covered, someone needs a signature, the town manager requires reports, the state library wants statistics. These activities should be considered a role, and resources should be set aside for administrative tasks.

If a library has the resources (that is, it is not a bare bones operation struggling to keep the doors open) it may also select a third, minor role in addition to its primary and secondary role. But beware of trying to stretch the library's resources too thin. It is better to do two things well than to attempt to do half a dozen things half way.

DPL's MINOR ROLE

There was no getting around it, people really like the library's reading readiness program for preschoolers. The parents of young children had come to depend on the story hours and teddy bear picnics. The elementary school teachers said that they could always tell which kids had been library regulars. This seemed so important to the planning committee that they decided that the library should have as its minor role, *services to preschoolers*.

The roles that you select for your library, and the order in which you rank them, will help you to allocate the available money, people, and time. If your primary role is "Preschoolers' Door to Learning," and your secondary role is "Popular Materials Library," you would fund the story hour before buying extra copies of the hot new bestseller; and you would buy the bestseller before updating the expensive reference source that is only out-of-date by a year. If "Reference Library" is a relatively important minor role, you might update the reference source before buying the GED study guides that would support the less important minor role of "Formal Education Support Center."

In practice, it may be hard to tell where one role leaves off, and another role begins. When the local author speaks at the library, the program could contribute to the roles of "Community Activities

Center" (all those people came to the library) or "Independent Learning Center" (and they learned about how an author came to write a book). It is more important to have a general understanding of what your library's major and minor roles are, and how these roles relate to one another, than it is to precisely catalog each and every one of your activities.

Sometimes libraries undertake large and extraordinary projects. The most common projects are aimed at automation (either circulation and/or the catalog and technical services) or renovation of the library's building. These types of undertakings can be both exciting and overwhelming. Libraries contemplating building or automation projects should have a clear understanding of both the library's overall mission, as well as the specific roles that the library plays. These projects should be considered in the light of your major roles. In a library that is a "Popular Materials Library" an automated circulation system is more important than renovated meeting space. If library usage has increased to the point that there is no room for the school kids to do their homework, and your primary role is "Formal Education Support Center," than the addition of a new wing is imperative if you are to fill both that role and, ultimately, your mission. Remember, the point of building or automating is not to have a new building or a computer, but to better serve the community.

ALLOCATING RESOURCES

No doubt about it, selecting roles and creating priorities is difficult. These steps, so critical to the overall plan, require confronting the ugly reality of limited resources. It only gets harder. Resources—time, people, and money and the odd way that they are all tied together—have to be allocated. But, as this is a long-range plan, we can still afford to be fairly general with our numbers. Remember, these are ballpark figures, not hard and fast percentages to be applied across the board to the book budget, staff hours, or space allotment. All we are saying here is that 50 percent of our efforts will be aimed at our primary role and 30 percent to our secondary role.

FIGURE 6-2: **Danville Public Library-Defining Roles**

Danville Public Library Roles

Primary role

The library is a center for independent and assisted learning.

This role will require approximately 45 percent of the library's resources.

Secondary role

The library is a source of support for the grade school students of Danville.

This role will require approximately 20 percent of the library's resources.

Minor role

The library provides services to preschoolers.

This role will require approximately 15 percent of the library's resources.

Administrative role

This role will require approximately 20 percent of the library's resources.

FIGURE 6-3: **One Shot/Low Maintenance Projects**

Danville Public Library
One Shot/Low Maintenance Projects

Project	Assignment
Community Information Sheet	Assistant Librarian to gather data this March. Update annually.
Services to scholars	Refer to the library at the State University, state historical society or state library. DPL librarians should meet w/ librarians from these institutions informally at annual state library association convention to establish & maintain contact.

SUGGESTED READINGS

Without question, the place to start considering the roles of the public library is with *Planning & Role Setting for Public Libraries* (Chicago: American Library Association, 1987). Written for the Public Library Development Project, this manual details the resources needed for a library to fill a given role. (Available from the American Library Association, 50 E. Huron Street, Chicago, IL 60611 (800) 545-2433, ex. 1540.)

Two examples of how libraries selected their roles, and then put those roles into action are described in the following articles:

- "Upgrading the McLibrary," by Nancy Pearl and Craig Buthold. *Library Journal*, October 15, 1992, pp. 37-39.

- "Shhh! Kids and Scholars at Work," by Bruce Weber. *New York Times Magazine*, September 23, 1990, pp. 47+.

REFERENCES

1. *The 1992 Annual Report*. The New York Public Library.
2. Weber, Bruce. "Shhh! Kids and Scholars at Work." *New York Times Magazine*, September 23, 1990, pp. 47+.
3. "Birmingham Library Retargets Audience." *Library Journal*, March 25, 1990, p. 16.
4. Pearl, Nancy and Craig Buthod. "Upgrading the 'McLibrary.'" *Library Journal*, October 15, 1992, p. 39.
5. *Minutes*. Richards Free Library Trustees meeting, February 17, 1992.
6. "Study Says Half of Adults in U.S. Can't Read or Handle Arithmetic." *The New York Times*, September 9, 1993, p. 1.

WORKSHEET DIRECTIONS

Worksheet 6-1
Using your library's mission statement, and the impressions and the data gathered during the inventory, select, and define your library's roles, and allocate resources to those roles.

Worksheet 6-2
For your library's "leftover" roles, set up one shot/low maintenance projects.

WORKSHEET 6-1: The Library's Roles

Primary role:

This role will require approximately _____ % of the library's resources.

Secondary role:

This role will require approximately _____ % of the library's resources.

Minor role:

Approximate allocation of resources

Administration

20 percent (Administrative Functions)

WORKSHEET 6-2: One Shot/ Low Maintenance Projects

Project	**Assignment**

7 SETTING GOALS AND TARGETING OBJECTIVES

Having defined the roles that your library is to play in your community, the planning committee must now begin to grapple with the specific ways in which the library will fill these roles. Using the idealism of the mission statement, and the focus of the library's roles as a springboard, the library is preparing to leap into action.

It is all very well and good to say that the library's primary role is to be a "doorway to learning," but how exactly will the library act out this role? How will we know if the library is successful, that it is indeed a doorway to learning or a popular material center, or whatever we have decided on as a role? We must further define our role, breaking it down into more exact goals.

SETTING GOALS

Looking at your library's major roles, what should the library be doing? Don't get too exact yet, that comes later. What general goals should the library try to reach? Each role may require several goals. For example, at a library which has defined its major role to be a preschoolers doorway to learning, the goals should:

- provide materials and services to preschoolers,

- provide a source of information and support to the parents of preschoolers, and

- create a place where preschoolers come to learn.

TARGETING OBJECTIVES

Once you have determined the goals that will lead to filling your library's roles, you are ready to target definite objectives. The defining feature of an objective is that it can be measured. An objective is just that, objective. By establishing precise objectives, you have a way to measure your success. We can argue a subjective point, such as weather or not the library is successful at providing materials and services to preschoolers. But we have a harder time arguing the facts. If over the last year circulation of the children's collection has increased by 25 percent and attendance at story hour is up by 56 percent, it is easier to determine if the library is meeting its goal of providing materials and services to preschoolers. If a library is meeting its goals, then it must be filling its role, and therefore, it is a little further down the road to fulfilling its mission.

A single goal may have several objectives. To continue the example of preschoolers doorway to learning, if the goal is to provide materials and services to preschoolers, than the objectives that would support that goal might be:

- to increase story hour attendance by 75 percent by the end of the planning period,

- to increase the circulation of the children's collection by 50 percent over the next five years, and

- to meet annually with primary grade school teachers to gage our effectiveness.

ACTIVITIES

Each of these objectives, in turn, requires specific activities. It is by undertaking these activities that you will accomplish your objectives. In order to increase circulation, the library may have to buy more children's books, create bibliographies for parents who want to read to their children, and put up eye catching displays in the children's room. To increase story hour attendance may mean that the library must renovate the children's room and add another part-time children's librarian to the staff. Each activity should have a deadline.

TASKS

A single activity may require a series of tasks. If the library is to renovate the children's room, then money must be set aside by the town, grants need to be written, an architect must be hired, contractors interviewed, and so on. Tasks should also have deadlines.

How responsibility for a task or activity is assigned depends on a library's specific circumstances and the nature of the assignment. A committee could be put in charge of automation, building renovations or other major activities that require a multitude of tasks and the work of a lot of different people. An activity may be the responsibility of several groups or individuals. The Board of Trustees, the automation committee, and the library director and staff might all share responsibility working closely together to implement an upgrade of the library's computer. If it is clear who is in charge of what tasks, you don't have to explicitly state this joint responsibility. Assume cooperation.

When you assign someone the responsibility of carrying out a task or activity, you must also give them the authority that they will need to complete the assignment. If you ask me to do something, I am going to need resources (time, people, and money) to carry out my charge. I am also going to need to understand what you expect me to do, when this is to be done by, and how what I am doing fits into the library's overall plan.

A single goal will generate several objectives. A single objective may generate many activities and tasks. In addition to spelling out the library's goals and objectives, the plan should also prioritize the library's objectives.

Therefore, the role of "Preschoolers Doorway to Learning" would lead to a set of goals, objectives, activities, and tasks like this:

Goal: To provide materials and services to preschoolers.

First Objective: To increase story hour attendance 75 percent by the end of the planning period.

Activity: In order to seat more children, there is a need to renovate the children's room. (Completed in the winter of year five)

Task: Board of Trustees (BOT) appoints building committee (next month)

Task: BOT asks that capital be set aside by town. (Spring, years 2-4)

Task: Library director oversees grant process. (Summer year 2 through Fall year 5)

Task: Building committee interviews architects/BOT hires. (Fall year 2)

Second Objective: To increase the circulation of the children's collection by 50 percent over the next 5 years.

Activity: Hire second part-time librarian. (Spring, year 2)

Task: Money voted by town (Spring, year 2)

Task: Fill position.(Spring, year 2)

Activity: Improve the children's collection (Spring year 3)

Task: Children's librarian and library director weed the children's collection (Fall year 2)

Task: Children's librarian compares collection with appropriate bibliography and compiles acquisition list (Spring, year 3) and so on.

Timeline Display

Activities and tasks can also be displayed on a timeline, showing the beginning of a project, its duration, and the completion date (see Figure 7-1). When the library's one-shot, low-maintenance projects are added to this timeline, it is possible to know, month by month, what the library should be doing in order to make all this come true. These timelines can be quite elaborate and detailed. If you use a timeline, don't make it any more complicated than you have to. It is a graphic representation, not an end unto it self.

The timing of your objectives is important. By telling the town, "In five years we are going to need an addition," and then, "In four years we are going to need an addition," "In three years . . . ," etc., people are better prepared to fund the addition than if you sprang it on them all at once.

MULTIPLE OBJECTIVES

Some activities may contribute to meeting more than one objective. In the above example, hiring a children's librarian will help increase both story hour attendance and the circulation of the children's collection. It doesn't really matter if this activity goes under one objective or the other. In fact, this is exactly the kind of situation you want to create with your plan—all the activities, all the tasks, all the goals and roles seem to be related. All that you are doing has a focus or central theme.

Most likely, your objectives will require additional funding. If that funding is not forthcoming, the objective cannot be met. Try to create some objectives that can be accomplished with no additional funding. This way, even if additional money is not forthcoming, the library can make some progress towards its goals. Build success into the plan.

Doing without is a dangerous game. Public libraries have traditionally been underfunded. When our budgets are cut we make do

FIGURE 7-1:

	December year 1	December year 2	December year 3	December year 4	December year 5
Activity					
Children's room renovation					X
Tasks					
Building committee appointed	X				
Capital set aside		X	X	X	X
Grant process		O ———————————————X			
Hire architect	O ———X				
Activity					
Improve children's collection	O ———————————————X				
Tasks					
Hire pt librarian	O———X				
Weed collection		O ————————X			
Create acq. list		O ————————X			

Key
O = start
——— = duration
X = completion

Notes:

_____

_____

_____

_____

_____

_____

_____

and carry on as best we can. Because there is no outcry, no threat to public safety (remember Maslow's theory), the next time there is a short fall, the budget-makers will again look to the library. By having clearly stated goals and objectives, you have something to point to when the budget battles are being fought (i.e., If we don't have X dollars, then we cannot achieve these objectives). If the goals and objectives are grounded in the community's needs, it makes it that much harder for the budget-cutters to come after the library.

Objectives have a way of making people nervous. There they are, for all the world to see: the target that you are expected to hit. If circulation doesn't go up by 50 percent, that's it, you have failed. What if circulation only goes up by 45 percent? It may not be exactly on target, but it is still a respectable showing. What if circulation goes up by 40 percent or 35 percent? The point is that, with some objectives, even if you achieve only half of what you set out to do, you are still half again better off then if you had done nothing at all.

Objectives should be used to motivate people, not frighten them. At this stage of the planning process, the planning committee will want to consult closely with members of the library staff and the board of trustees. Ask them if they think that the objectives outlined in the plan are reasonable. "We think that the library can increase circulation by 50 percent over the next five years. Do you think that this is an attainable objective? Do you have any suggestions on how we can achieve this?" These are the people who are going to do the work; they need a voice in how it will be done.

Focus on the activities that will be undertaken in the first two years of the plan. For some objectives you may not know what activities will be effective in three or four years. Activities for the six months or year ahead could be a topic covered in the review process.

Since Chapter 8 is a detailed examination of library statistics, you will want to study it closely as you target objectives for your library. In the early stages of implementing the plan, keep the statistics low key and simple. Let people get comfortable using statistics as a means of management.

DANVILLE'S GOALS AND OBJECTIVES

Role: The library is a center for independent and assisted learning.

Goal: To serve all the people of Danville.

Objective: To increase the number of registered borrowers to 85 percent of the town's population.

Deadline: By the end of year three.

Activity: Create and maintain an aggressive outreach program.

Goal: To help people learn new job skills or make career changes.

Objective: To increase the use of the job hunting/job skill collection by 25 percent.

Deadline: By the end of year 4.

Activity: Weed current collection; identify and procure needed items.

Activity: Hold monthly job hunting and resume writing workshops.

Activity: Start an adult literacy program.

Goal: To inspire or rekindle a love of learning.

Objective: Increase circulation by 15 percent.

Deadline: By the end of year four.

Activity: Work with local schools, bookstores, and newspapers to create an annual "Week Without Television."

Activity: Produce a series of popular materials (Mysteries, Romances, Westerns, Thrillers) bibliographies that lead users deeper into the library's collection. (If you like Stephen King, try Edgar Allen Poe; If you like Edith Wharton, try Henry James.)

Activity: Create a new book display area near the circulation desk.

Objective: To establish book discussion groups.

Deadline: By the end of year five.

Role: The library is a source of support for grade school students.

Goal: To provide an after school learning environment.

Objective: Involve 50 percent of the town's grade school students in after school programs.

Deadline: By the end of year five.

Activity: Refurbish basement storeroom as quiet study area.

Activity: Work with middle school teachers to establish homework help program.

DANVILLE'S OBJECTIVES RANKED IN ORDER OF IMPORTANCE

First objective: Increase the number of registered borrowers to 85 percent of the town's population.

Second objective: Increase use of job hunting/job skills collection by 25 percent.

Third objective: Increase circulation by 15 percent.

Fourth objective: Involve 50 percent of the town's grade school students in after school programs.

Fifth objective: Establish book discussion groups.

DIRECTIONS FOR THE WORKSHEET

Taking your roles, what are your goals? How is your library going to act out its mission? What are your specific objectives? Once these issues have been decided, the planning committee should sit down with the Board of Trustees and the library staff to determine:

1. realistic objectives,

2. productive activities, and

3. a list of tasks.

Then, rank your library's objectives in order of their importance.

WORKSHEET 7-1: Role Defining Worksheet

Role:

Goal:

Objective:

Activity:

Task 1:

Task 2:

Task 3:

Objective:

Activity:

Task 1:

Task 2:

Task 3:

KEEPING SCORE

Why keep statistics? Tracking the number of books that are checked out and reference questions asked is time consuming and inconvenient. The results, a collection of dry numbers, may not seem worth the trouble. Yet statistics, if carefully gathered and artfully arranged, can measure a library's progress in transforming the vision of the mission into an every day reality. In short, what we are trying to do with library statistics is to take measure of our success.

Numbers are a way to demonstrate, to prove or disprove, what we intuit. Numbers are a way to record the minute particulars of day-to-day activities. In moving a library forward, numbers are performance targets.

Numbers are more specific than words. In conversation, we say things like "The house cost a lot of money" and "I was chased by a lot of angry bees," in the first instance, "a lot" means thousands; in the other, it may mean as little as three.

Expressing performance with concrete numbers often helps those who are unfamiliar with the library to understand the scope of the library's activities. Saying that 57 percent of the town's population attended a program at the library last year puts something that the library does into terms that anyone can understand.

Numbers allow for comparisons, both to your library's past and projected performance, and to other libraries. Consider the example shown in Figure 8-1: There are seven libraries participating in the Smith County Co-op. The Dedham Library is by far the highest circulating library; with the exception of the Grant Library, Chatham has the lowest circulation. Yet, by putting their numbers in comparative terms, we see that Chatham's circulation skyrocketed by about 15 percent each year—a rate that is three times the Co-op's overall growth rate of five percent. While these figures certainly give the Chatham Library something to crow about, they also prompt the question, "What's that little library in Chatham doing that juices up circulation?" These types of comparisons can also help to allocate resources and cost. Since the Smith County Co-op shares an automated circulation system, Chatham's apportionment was increased. With the increased revenues, the Co-op purchased an additional hard drive to accommodate Chatham's increased demand on the system.

In making an item-by-item comparison of your library and even its most similar peer, you will see a thousand and one variables. They have more children in their town, so their circulation figures are higher. We have a bigger parking lot so more people attend our programs. When looking closely at a neighboring library's statistics,

FIGURE 8-1: **Smith Country Library Co-op Comparative Statistics—Circulation**

	1991	1992	Change (%)	1993	Change (%)
Akron	85,583	83,189	-2.80	77,370	-6.99
Bethesda	113,686	115,555	1.64	118,933	2.92
Chatham	26,378	30,130	14.22	35,311	17.20
Dedham	330,081	351,790	6.58	377,411	7.28
Essex	137,943	152,246	10.37	166,293	9.23
Farmington	95,014	99,274	4.48	101,400	2.14
Grant	NA	NA		9,000	
Total Circ	788,685	832,184	5.52	876,718	5.35

apply what you know to what you observe. Knowing that Dedham has a lot of young families, when you look at Dedham's annual circulation figures, are you surprised?

Declining numbers are not necessarily bad news. The drop in the Akron Library's circulation may be the result of a change in the length of their borrowing period. Akron's falling circulation may be the result of a demographic changes, a decline in the overall population, the opening of the nearby Grant Library, or an increase in library program attendance may have come at the expense of circulation. Library statistics can be used as a starting point for discussion and self appraisal. "Our circulation figures were down last year, but reference questions were up. Why is that?"

There is a saying among those who work with computers, "Garbage in, garbage out." If you put garbage, that is, poor data, into a computer, you will get garbage, or poor results, out of the computer. The same principal applies here. The better the numbers that you put into an equation, the more accurate the picture of the library and its services.

Define your terms.

It is important that everyone who counts reference questions agrees on what is and what isn't a reference question. At children's programs, are adults who sit in included in the tally of attenders? Try to be consistent. Keep a statistics notebook in which you record your definitions and explain how your library gathers its numbers. You will also want to note variables, like the week last summer when the library's parking lot was closed because it was being repaved, or the year program attendance was way down because the high school girls basketball team was state champion, and everyone was at the games, the pep rallies, and the victory parade.

PRACTICAL CONSIDERATIONS

Make sure that you prioritize your actions. For instance, tailor your statistics gathering to your roles. If your library is a Popular Materials Center, then the circulation figures would be more important than reference numbers. At the Community Activity Center library, the attendance count at a programmed event would be taken more carefully and scrutinized closer than circulation numbers. In a Reference Center, more time and detail would be devoted to reference statistics. With all these statistics, you will need to find your "comfort level." You will have to determine just how accurate your statistics have to be. In some areas, you will be as accurate as possible. In others you may be happy with being somewhere in the ball park.

DANVILLE'S IMPORTANT STATISTICS

The ranking of Danville's objectives determined the library's important statistics.

First objective: To increase the number of registered borrowers to 85 percent of the town's population.

Second objective: Increase use of job hunting/job skills collection by 25 percent.

Third objective: Increase circulation by 15 percent.

Fourth objective: Involve 50 percent of the town's grade school students in after school programs.

Fifth objective: Establish book discussion groups.

So, the most important statistic will be borrowers as a percentage of population, followed by in-house use and circulation of the job hunting collection, overall circulation, and program participation.

Make gathering numbers as easy as possible. Post tally sheets where they can be seen and used. It may be easier for each staff member to keep their own, individual tally sheet. This way you don't have to fight your way past another staffer, working right where you need to be to make your mark on the one and only tally sheet. One of the most practical ways to keep track of what you have done in a given day is to carry a small pad of paper around and jot down call numbers, page references, and telephone messages as you go. At the end of the day you can sit down and count it all up. (A jack pad is a bit more elaborate than a pad of paper. It consists of a small leather wallet with a pocket that holds 3 x 5 cards on one side and a storage pocket on the other. After making brief notations on the cards, it is easy to slip the old cards into the pocket. At the end of the day, review the cards and tally up.)

The following tally sheets (Figures 8-2 through 8-4) for circulation, reference and programming show the level of detail that a library can go into in gathering what it considers its most important statistics.

Total up the tally sheets once a week and report the weekly and year-to-date results regularly to the people who are helping you to gather these numbers. Do all that you can to dispel the impression that record keeping is trivial busy work.

PERFORMANCE MEASURES

The Danville Public Library Statistics for 1991 through 1993 (see Figure 8-5) show how a library can chart its performance over time. Using the 1993 figures as an example, let us look at some of the different ways to measure library activity. (The answers are in the appendix of DPL's final report in Chapter 9.)

Registered Borrowers as a Percent of Population

What does it mean when you say "Our library has 5,872 registered patrons?" Is 5,872 a lot or only a few? That depends whether your library serves a community of 9,000 people or 100,000. This is what we are getting at when we calculate the borrowers as a percentage of the population ratio.

FIGURE 8-2: **Reference Tally Sheet**

Date:

Number of reference questions asked:

The Results

Answered on the spot:

Call back—question required in depth research:

Beyond our understanding:

You may wish to provide a detailed description of a Remarkable Reference Transaction (a rousing success, a dismal failure, an unbelievable question, etc.). Remarkable Reference Transactions may be discussed at the monthly Reference Staff meeting.

FIGURE 8-3: Circulation Report

Date:

	Adult	**YA**	**Children**
Fiction			
Total			
Non fiction			
000-199			
200- 299			
300-399			
400-499			
500-599			
600-699			
700-799			
800-899			
900-999			
Total			

CD's

Rock	**Folk**	**Jazz**	**Classical**	**Other**

Total

Videos

Total

Reminder: Please tell the acquisition librarian of items that have more than 5 people on the waiting list. Thanks!

FIGURE 8-4: **Program Attendance**

Program Attendance

Date & Time:

Title:

Intended audience:

Anticipated attendance:

Refreshments served Y/N ?

Please outline any and all pre-program publicity:

Actual attendance:

Other comments:

FIGURE 8-5: Danville Public Library Statistics

Danville Public Library
Library Statistics

	1991	1992	1993
Registered borrowers	5863	5872	5879
Population	9024	9068	9068
Borrowers as % of Population	64.9	64.7	
Circulation	77,370	10,368	113,380
Circulation/capita	8.57	11.6	
Reference	7228	8110	7814
Reference/capita	.80	.861	
Program attendance	1828	3526	2327
Program/capita	.202	.388	.256
Number of vol's	36,402	41,343	44,824
Turnover	2.12	2.54	

Registered Borrowers

How many people are card-carrying library users? Of course, this number is meaningful only if your patron files are accurate. Weed out those who have died or moved. If you are checking books out on their parents' cards for children who can sign their names, consider issuing cards to the children.

Population

Who are you obligated to serve? Some libraries have either formal or informal arrangements to serve certain portions of the population who may fall outside their strictly defined legal service area. If you extend borrowing privileges to the residents of an unincorporated township on the other side of the county line, or to the kids from out of town who attend the regional high school across the street, be sure to include these folks in your population figure. Of course, you should use the most recent and accurate numbers that are available. This population figure is the keystone in library statistics.

To find a percentage generally, divide the part by the whole and then multiply by 100. To find what percent of the population are registered library borrowers, divide the number of borrowers (part) by the whole population, then multiply by 100. In a town with a population of 9,068, and registered borrowers of 5,879 the math looks like this:

$$5879 \div 9068 = .648$$
$$648 \times 100 = 64.8\%$$

Is 64 percent more or less than the prior year? You can compare your current statistics to past performance, as well as to the performance of a peer group (that is, the group of local libraries that are most like your library in terms of size and demographics).

Per capita comparisons

Performance for most areas of library activities can best be measured in terms of per capita ratios. That is, the number of items circulated, reference questions asked, and so on are divided by the number of people in the user population.

Circulation

A book, video, or CD is checked out of the library by a borrower. The library records the borrower, the item, and the due date. The borrower leaves with the item and returns it before it is due, after it is due, or whenever. That is one circulation transaction. If the borrower renews a loan, that is considered another, second circulation transaction. The longer the borrowing period, the lower the circulation figures. Time is a factor in figuring annual circulation statistics—the more available due dates, the greater the number of opportunities for circulation activities.

Circulation per capita

Divide circulation (the part) by population (the whole). In a town of 9,068, with circulation of 113,380, do the following division:

$$113,380 \div 9068 = 12.5$$

In other words, every member of the town borrows twelve and a half items per year from the library. Circulation per capita is important to Popular Materials libraries.

Reference questions

What is a reference question? Everyone who tracks reference questions needs to be able to distinguish between directional and procedural questions (Where is the photocopying machine? If a book isn't on the shelf, how can I get hold of it?) and reference questions (I'm planning a trip to Switzerland, what is the weather like there? I'm doing a paper on Benjamin Franklin). Sometimes staff members who may not be official "reference librarians" answer reference questions. Make sure that the reference questions that they answered are included in the reference tally.

Reference questions per capita

Divide the number of reference questions (the part) per year by population (the whole).

$$7814 \div 9068 = .861$$

Since the answer is less than one, and a statement like "every man, woman, and child in this town asked eight-tenths of a reference question last year" is likely to cause confusion, change the figure to a percentage.

$$.861 \times 100 = 86.1\%$$

86 percent of the town's population asked a reference question that year. Reference Libraries and Community Information Center Libraries would carefully track this statistic.

PROGRAM ATTENDANCE

Do you count the people as they come in, as they sit through the program, or as they leave? At a children's program, do you count the parents who stay for the program?

Program attendance per capita

Divide attendance by population.

$$2327 \div 9068 = .256$$

Again, express this number as a percentage of population.

$$.256 \times 100 = 25.6\%$$

25 percent of the town attended a program at the library that year. Program attendance per capita is an important statistic at Community Activity Center Libraries.

NUMBER OF VOLUMES

The rule of thumb is that every inch of shelflist cards represents approximately 100 books. Using this standard, it is easy to get a rough idea of the size of the library's collection. However, there are some other factors that you may wish to take into consideration. In this set of exercises, we will be using the number of volumes figure to determine the scope of the collection. The number of volumes should include any and all items that can be checked out of the library. If certain parts of your collection can not be taken from the library (parts of the reference section, bound magazines, magazines on micro fiche or film), these items should not be included in the number of volumes tally. If single issues of a magazine circulate, you can figure out how many issues you have by the magazine's frequency. *Time* magazine appears 50 times a year. An annual subscription to *Time* adds 50 items to the number of volumes count. You may wish to calculate the number of volumes several ways—the number of circulating volumes (or, more accurately, circulating items), the number of volumes excluding magazines, and the total number of volumes (circulating and non-circulating). The number that you use depends on what you are trying to show. To demonstrate circulation performance, use the number of circulating items. To show the need for an addition to the building, compare the total number of volumes per square foot of library space.

TURNOVER

Turnover measures how many times a year an item is borrowed from the library. Some items are checked out of the library many times each year, and others may not go out at all (i.e., wallflower books). Turnover won't show the strengths and weaknesses of a library's collection, but it provides an overall view of the use of materials. A high turnover rate is a sign that a library is actively collecting the types of materials that its patrons want. To determine the rate, divide circulation (the part), by the number of volumes (the whole).

$$113,380 \div 44,824 = 2.52$$

Turnover is important at Popular Materials Libraries.

OTHER MEASURES

There are a seemingly endless variety of performance measures that you can apply to your library. It is possible to calculate everything from circulation per staff member to the number of homework related questions per students K through 12. Be clear on what you are trying to demonstrate with your numbers. Use numbers to help people to better understand just what it is that the library does.

Sampling

One popular way to gather library statistics is to take a sampling of various library activities. There are a number of ways to go about sampling, but all involve a fair amount of effort and, as with all sampling methods, the results are open to interpretation. The statistics discussed earlier in this chapter are enumerative, that is, they are derived by counting each and every time an item is checked out, a reference question is asked, or someone attends a program. Sampling requires that selections be made. Which week will we conduct a users survey? What if the weather is awful that week? What about the users that don't come to the library that week? What about the nonusers, or the folks who don't have time to answer our questions? What questions should we ask and how shall we phrase them? ("How can library services be improved?" is a very difficult question to answer. It is far easier to answer "Which would you rather have, expanded children's services or an increase in the adult non-fiction collection?") Yet as messy as sampling is, it can be used to gage user preference and satisfaction.

Surveys are visible to patrons: When you approach someone with the intention of asking their opinion, you are asking for their time and thought. Make sure that your canvassers understand this and are prepared to listen politely to even the most bizarre suggestions. Report the survey results back to your patrons. This could be done with a handout at the circulation desk, a brief article in the local paper, or a paragraph in the library's annual report.

A survey can be conducted over the telephone, through the mail, or face-to-face, either at the library or at another location: With a telephone survey, there is the ever-present threat of interrupting someone as they sit down to eat, have one foot out the door, or are waiting to hear if it is a boy or a girl. Surveys done through the mail usually have very poor rates of return. Plainly, face-to-face surveys done at the library capture the feelings of library users. Standing outside the super market may be a way to reach non-users.

In designing a survey, consider what percentage of the population you actually want to talk to: The larger the total population, the smaller the percentage that can be directly contacted. Also, think about when the survey will be taken. For face-to-face surveys, pick a typical day or week at the library—a time that is neither in the dead of winter, nor the heat of summer (unless, you serve a seasonal community and want to study the seasonal fluctuations), when school is in session, and there are no big, three-day weekends coming up.

Before starting out with a clipboard, know exactly what questions you want to ask and how you are going to ask them. If people have trouble answering, think about how you phrase your questions. Be sure to briefly explain any technical terms. You may want to omit the behind the scene details. Most people have only an inkling of what goes on in the backroom of a library and mid-survey is not the time to enlighten them.

Fill rates

Fill rates are gathered by doing an in-house, face-to-face survey. Fill rates show the likelihood of a patron walking into the library with a particular author, title, or subject area in mind, and finding what they want. As the patron exits the library, a canvasser asks if they came to the library wanting something in particular, and if so, did they find it. In addition to author, title, and subject fill rates, there is the browsing fill rate. This measures the success rate of folks when they come to the library and browse for a "good read."

Here's how the title fill rate works:
Each of the following transactions begins with the canvasser asking: "Did you come to the library today looking for something specific?"

Transaction 1:
Patron replies: "Yes. I was looking for *Gone with the Wind*."
Canvasser asks: "Did you find it?"
Patron: "Yes."

Transaction 2:
Patron replies: "Yes. I was looking for *War and Peace*."
Canvasser asks: "Did you find it?"
Patron: "No, but they said that they would get it for me."

Transaction 3:
Patron replies: "I was looking for something by Tony Hillerman."

	Was a specific title needed?	Was that title on hand?
Transaction 1	Yes	Yes
Transaction 2	Yes	No
Transaction 3	No (this transaction doesn't count in the title fill rate tally).	

For each column, let yes answers equal one while no answers equal zero. From these values calculate the titles needed and the titles on hand.

$$\text{titles needed} = 2$$
$$\text{titles on hand} = 1$$

Divide the number of titles on hand (the part) by the number of titles needed (the whole).

$$1 \div 2 = .5$$

To express this as a percentage, multiply by 100.

$$.5 \times 100 = 50\%$$

The library's title fill rate is 50 percent.

Different libraries will be more or less interested in different fill rates. A Popular Materials library might combine author and title fill rates. This way, if a patron replies, "I was looking for *Devises and Desires* by P.D. James which isn't on the shelf. But I did find *Innocent Blood*," the transaction would be included in an author/title tally. This approach, however, wouldn't be useful in a Formal Education Support library. A copy of *War & Peace* is of no use to a student looking for *Anna Karenina*.

Measuring in-house use

One way for library to gage the effectiveness of its collection involves sampling the in-house use of the collection. During a typical, pre-determined day (or week) patrons would be asked to return items that they used while in the library to a designated spot. From there the items would be counted and then reshelved. If the tally is 500 items and the library is open 300 days a year, then:

$$500 \times 300 = 150,000 \text{ items used per year.}$$

If the collection is 45,000 volumes, dividing the part (number of items used) by the whole (number of volumes) gives you the average amount of times a specific volume is used every year.

$$150,000 \div 45,000 = 3.33$$

Every volume in the library is used 3.33 times a year. Since this statistic doesn't include items that a patron takes out, fill rates are not particularly important to Popular Materials Libraries, but very important to Reference Libraries.

COMPARATIVE STATISTICS

Another helpful way to view your library's statistics is in comparison with other libraries' numbers. While there are endless possibilities for comparisons, keep in mind that the larger the sampling pool that you use, the less glaring are the aberrations in the underlaying assumptions (they have a longer loan period, we serve more children, etc.). The annual library statistical reports issued by state library organizations are an outstanding source for state wide statistics.

SUGGESTED READING

Output Measures for Public Libraries: A manual for standardized procedures, second edition (Chicago: American Library Association, 1987).

DIRECTIONS FOR THE WORKSHEETS

Worksheet 8-1

Before tackling Worksheet 8-1, consider the following questions. Looking at your library's roles, what are the most important statistics for your library? What are the less important statistics? How are statistics gathered at your library? Can your data collecting methods be improved or simplified?

Using the following worksheet, compare your library's performance over the past three years.

WORKSHEET 8-1   Library Statistics

	Year 1	Year 2	Year 3
Registered borrowers			
Population			
Borrowers as % of Population			
Circulation			
Circulation/capita			
Reference			
Reference/capita			
Program attendance			
Program/capita			
Number of vol's			
Turnover			

9 WRITING THE PLAN

At last, you're nearing the end of the planning process. The Committee is exhausted. The staff is tired of hearing about and working on "the plan." When will the process finally be over and the plan implemented? Let's stop all this talk and just do it.

It is tempting to skip committing the final version of the plan to paper. Writing is a difficult and time consuming task. Yet, clear writing is often evidence of clear thinking. Writing out the plan is one last opportunity to think the plan—the assumptions, the numbers, the conclusions—all the way through. At this point, it is easy to remember all the details, the timetables, and assignments. A year from now, 365 days into the action, these things will not be as easy to recall. Take the time to write, edit, produce, and distribute a written plan.

FIRST IMPRESSIONS ARE LASTING

Be sure that the final draft of the plan that you distribute looks presentable. A report produced on a personal computer hooked to a laser or ink jet printer simply looks better than something banged out on a manual typewriter and then mimeographed. If you can't afford to have the report professionally printed, use the best means of reproduction that you have available.

Little things mean a lot. Have several people proofread for spelling and meaning. Explain any and all technical terms and acronyms. Most people have very little idea of what goes on behind the scenes in a library.

One member of the planning committee can author the report and submit drafts to the committee for their comments and approval. On the other hand, as editing is easier than writing, each member of the committee could be assigned to write a section, with one member editing the sections together.

EXPECT SOME DISAGREEMENT

By this point, the plan is nearly complete, in print, and more or less exactly what the library intends to do. Some committee members (or staff members) may feel that not enough is being done about X, and Y is simply out of the question. It is unlikely that everyone is going to be in perfect agreement on every aspect of the plan. Aim for a consensus that the plan, as a whole, is something everyone can live with.

As you sit down to write, ask yourself, "Who is my audience?" For the library director, staff, and trustees the statistics, demographics, and projections form the framework for the library's activities of the next several years. But what about everyone else? How are the aldermen, the budget committee, library users, and non-users going to find out about the library's plans? No matter how well it is written, most folks aren't going to read the entire report. Write a short, one-page summary that covers the basic who, what, why, when, where, and hows of your plan. Hand it out at the circulation desk. Send it to the local paper. Include a name and a phone number to call for more information. Somewhere in the summary, ask for the sale. (Any girl scout who has sold cookies door to door will tell you that there is a point when, after telling the potential customer that you in troop 314, and that the boxes are $3.00 each, you have to look them straight in the eye and say, "Would you like to buy some?" That is asking for the sale. In libraries this may translate to something like, "Come and discover the riches of your public library," or "The library needs your help! Vote to increase our funding.")

PARTS OF THE FINAL REPORT

The written plan is a chance to, step-by-step, and in plain view, build the case for what the committee is proposing. In rough political seas, the plan can be a raft to cling to. Each section of the report should be crafted to support the library's course of action. Write the report in a format that leads your reader gently, but inevitably towards your conclusions. Final reports usually include the following sections.

TITLE PAGE

Give your plan a title. It may be something as simple as "Looking Ahead: the Library's Five Year Plan." This way the planning committee, *not* someone else, has the opportunity to name what it is that they are proposing. You may want to use some form of your mission statement (or your mission truths) as your title. After all, this mission is what the plan is all about.

SUMMARY

This could be a modified version of your one-page summary. Remember that you have a relatively small amount of time to capture someone's attention. If you fail to get someone's attention, it is unlikely that you will win their vote. In the clearest possible manner, outline the who, what, why, when, where, and how of your plan. And remember, ask for the sale!

BACKGROUND AND OVERVIEW

Include a brief biography of who was on the planning committee, why this planning was undertaken, how the committee went about its work, who else helped out, what conclusions were reached, and what will happen next. The Introduction is really an expanded summary, but, if well written, it may lure the reader into the more substantive parts of the report that follow.

THE COMMUNITY AND THE LIBRARY

Report not only the results of the inventory, but also the reactions to the library and the impressions of the roles that it plays. If, as you talked to people, they were enthusiastic about the new book collection, or frustrated by the lack of parking, or wishing for more summer hours, record it in this section. Anecdotal evidence, while it doesn't take the place of hard numbers and cold facts, is often more compelling. Take every occasion to write about how the library helps people as they change careers, renovate their kitchens, read up on how to rear their kids, or contemplate the complexities of the universe.

THE LIBRARY'S MISSION AND ROLES, GOALS AND OBJECTIVES

Here is where you spell out the library's agenda and the rational behind it. Link the goals and objectives to the library's roles. Discuss how the library will put these roles into action. Reassure people that while the library has two major roles, it will still fill many of the functions it always has. List some of your proposed activities as examples.

THE REVIEW PROCESS

How are people going to know if the library accomplishes its objectives? The annual report, semi-annual newsletters, and press releases will do the job. Invite people to comment on the plan and offer ways for people to get involved with the library.

DISCUSSING COSTS AND FUNDING

"This is great, but who is going to pay for all this?" You can almost hear the selectman as he finishes reading the library's plan. You may or may not want to include the costs of the library's activities and potential sources of funding. You don't want to sink the plan at its very beginning ("$1.5 million! They have to be kidding! We can't raise that in five years!"). Also, you don't want to give out numbers that you may have to revise significantly later ("But you said in your report three years ago that this would only cost $1.5 million. Why are you asking for $2 million?). On the other hand, if the library is going to undertake a major (i.e., expensive) activity within the next year or two, it will have to be included in the budget. In this case, include at least a ballpark figure and suggest some funding sources. ("The renovations will cost approximately $10,000. State and federal grants may be available to fund this project.") Be sure to point out when something can be done with just a little additional funding.

Don't weight down your report with too much technical information. Present statistical tables in an appendix. You may want to refer people who are interested in extremely complicated information, such as the tabulation of survey results, to the library's reference desk. This way, you can make contact with these folks, and you can gently probe their interest in the library. Before starting, consult the sample plan included at the end of this Chapter.

SUGGESTED READING

When writing, keep in mind the advice of William Strunk and E.B. White. Their "little book," *The Elements of Style* (New York: MacMillan, 1972) is an excellent guide to composition, usage and grammar. It is exceptionally short, straightforward, and useful.

ENRICHING LIVES

THE DANVILLE PUBLIC LIBRARY

A PLAN FOR THE NEXT FIVE YEARS

Summary

In January 1993, at the request of the Board of Trustees of the Danville Public Library, a long range planning committee was formed. The Committee was given the charge of examining the mission of the library, the community that it serves, the roles that it plays, and how an already good library may become an excellent library

After studying these issues over the course of a year, the Planning Committee concluded that the library's overall mission remains unchanged from that envisioned by Miss Emma Crosswell, a early contributor to the library, in 1894. Miss Crosswell hoped that the library would "enrich the lives of others." What has changed is the nature of the community that the library serves. The increased demand for a trained, learned workforce and the profusion of entertainment options are both challenges that need to be addressed by the Danville Public Library. When it is reported that half of the adults in the United States can't read or handle arithmetic, these challenges are indeed formidable.

While the Danville Public Library offers many different services to many different patrons, the Committee suggests that the library focus on filling two major roles. The library should see itself as a center for independent and assisted learning, and as a center for support for the grade school students of Danville. In working towards filling these roles, the library has identified the following goals:

- Help people learn new job skills or make career changes.
- Inspire or rekindle a love of learning.
- Provide an after school learning environment for school children.

The library has also identified the following specific performance objectives that it hopes to achieve over the next five years.

- Increase use of job hunting/job skills collection by 25 percent.
- Increase circulation by 15 percent.
- Involve 50 percent of the town's grade school students in after school learning.
- Increase participation in book discussion groups by 40 percent.

The library director, staff, and Board of Trustees are committed to the continued success of the library in enriching lives. We ask the members of the Danville community to come and sample the treasures of *their* library. For more information, contact Philip Tullberg, Library Director, Danville Public Library, (Address/Phone number).

Background and Overview

In 1853, with a small appropriation of town monies and the donation of books by several prominent citizens, the Danville Public Library opened its doors. Housed in the basement of the old town hall, the library was open twelve hours a week, or by appointment, and citizens of good standing were allowed to borrow one book at a time.

With the generous bequest of $30,000 from Miss Emma Crosswell in 1894, the library was able to solve its pressing need for more space by constructing a new building on Front Street (the current site of the Danville Historical Society). The deed of Miss Crosswell's gift expressed the hope that the library would continue " . . . to enrich the lives of others as it done for me so often." In 1913, the Board of Trustees, noting a lack of space, voted to allow patrons to borrow two books at a time. It wasn't until 1942 that an addition, a separate children's room, could be built.

From 1965 to 1986, as holdings grew by a factor of four and the town's population almost doubled, the library proposed several different plans to alleviate the pressing need for more space. In the autumn of 1986, ground was broken on the banks of the Danville River for the new library building.

Today the library is busier than ever. Serving a population of almost 10,000 people, we circulate more than 113,000 books and answer 7800 reference questions a year. People of all ages attend lectures, movies, workshops, and story hours at the library. Using computers, the library can search electronic, on-line databases to locate and borrow books requested by users, or to research a topic. The library's collection of 430 compact discs and 500 videos are becoming increasingly popular.

A nine-member Board of Trustees is elected to oversee the library, establish policies and administer the budget. The Board also appoints the library director. The director and the library's staff of professional and paraprofessional personnel manage the day to day activities of the library. They are the ones who open the doors in the morning, put the books on the shelves, and answer the questions.

Most of the library's budget is appropriated by the town of Danville. Additional funds come through interest gained from the trust fund, donations, bequests, overdue fines, and the Friends of the Library book sale. These additional sources of income represent about 10 percent of the library's operating budget.

In January 1993, at the request of the Board of Trustees of the Danville Public Library, a long range planning committee was formed. The Committee was given the charge of examining the mission of the library, the community that it serves, the roles that it plays, and how better an already good library may become an excellent library

The planning committee was chaired by Joan Myers, a member of the Board of Trustees. Philip Tullberg, the library director, acted as secretary to the committee. Other committee members include:

- John Showalter, who retired last year after teaching physics at Danville High School for many years;

- Ann Neville, owner of Neville & Associates, graphic designers; and
- Karen Repoza, First shift supervisor, Danville Cordage Company and mother of Kevin and Keith Repoza, who were of invaluable assistance in helping the committee to better understand the needs of our grade school students.

The committee also wishes to thank the library staff, the Board of Trustees and the members of our community who helped us with their insight, suggestions and support.

The Community and the Library

The Community: Danville has a population of 9,068. Most people are between the ages of 18 and 65. Approximately 10 percent of the population is greater than 65, and another 10 percent are under 18. Danville has twice as many home owners as it does renters. The median house value is $154,000, and the median rent is $539. Housing stock includes both single and double family dwellings, apartments, condominiums, and manufactured housing. Danville's economy is a mix of light industry (Danville Cordage is the town's largest employer) and small retail and service businesses. Danville has an active chamber of commerce, and Rotary. Several years ago "the Cordage" cut its workforce by 15 percent. Some of the other smaller manufactures have also cut back on the number of people that they employ. While overall unemployment has held steady at a mild 4 percent, real earnings over the past ten years have also remained steady. In other words, everyone is just about holding their own, keeping up with inflation, but not making any real gains either.

The people of Danville have many educational and entertainment options. There are two elementary schools, one junior high, a public high school, a private high school, and a state supported community college. There are four child care centers and two nursery schools. There are two museums, a movie theater, a bowling alley, a country club, municipal tennis courts, golf course, swimming pool, and boat launch.

The Library: Approximately 65 percent of the town's population have library cards. Circulation is high. On a per capita basis, we circulate 12 and a half books to every man, woman, and child in Danville. (Complete library performance statistics may be found in Appendix A of this report.) While it appears that those who use the library are well served, more than a quarter of the town are not served by the library. Investigation shows that most of the 25 percent who do not use the library live west of the Danville River. The "West Side" has traditionally housed those that work at the Cordage. West Side residents report in interviews that they just never really consider coming to the library. They don't know that the library has a video or CD collection, that we have GED manuals, or that we have reading readiness story hours.

In conversations with the Library Director and staff members it was observed several times that the more popular items circulate at the most astonishing rates (for example, 65 people waiting to read a just published best selling potboiler). While not diminishing the importance of the library as a source of entertainment, there is concern that the library as a source of enlightenment is being overshadowed.

One of the perpetual complaints at the library is about the level of noise and activity generated by the junior high school students when they drop by after school. Interviews with members of that group revealed that "only a dweeb would use the school library." By virtue of the public library's proximity to the junior high, DPL is a study hall, resource center, tutoring center (kids report that there is usually one or two smart kids around who will explain an assignment or how to work an equation) and hang out for the "non-dweeb" set.

These are the challenges that the Danville Public Library faces. While at first glance it may seem daunting, we feel that these circumstances also offer the library the opportunity to grow and succeed in its mission.

The Library's Mission

It is the mission of the Danville Public Library to enrich lives. We offer our collection and services as a source of information, education, enlightenment, and entertainment, to all members of our community

The Library's Roles:

While the Danville Public Library plays many roles in the community, we believe that by focusing on two major roles we will be better able to achieve our mission. Our primary role is to be a center for independent and assisted learning. We also function as a source of support for the grade school students of Danville. The selection of these roles does not mean that the library will abandon its many other roles. There will still be services to preschoolers, and we will still be a source for popular materials. But much of what we do will be evaluated in terms of these two major roles.

The Library's Goals and Objectives

In order to focus the library's resources on fulfilling its two major roles, the Planning Committee, Trustees, and staff have identified the following goals and objectives to be worked toward over the next five years.

I. If the library is to be a center for independent and assisted learning, we must continue to bring people into the library. If they don't come in, we can't help them.

Goal: To serve all the people of Danville.

Objective: Increase the number of registered borrowers to 85% of the town's population.

Deadline: By the end of year three.

The library will undertake a number of activities to reach this objective. Under the direction of the library director, an aggressive outreach program will be launched, using all available media outlets to "get the word out" on what the library has to offer. The Trustees will investigate ways of reaching out to members of the business community.

II.   Noting the stale state of our economy, the library can be an important source of information on job skills training.

Goal: To help people learn new job skills or make career changes.

Objective: Increase the use of the job hunting/job skills collection by 25 percent.

Deadline: Spring, year four.

The collection will be weeded; needed materials identified and acquired. An increase in the book budget could accommodate these additional purchases without taking away from other areas.

III.   Education is a life-long process. Yet once one finishes one's formal education, the public library is one of the few institutions devoted to an individual, continued, life-long learning process.

Goal: To inspire or rekindle a love of learning.

First Objective: Increase circulation by 15 percent.

Deadline: By the end of year four.

Second Objective: Establish a book discussion group.

Deadline: By end of year two.

In coordination with local schools and bookstores, the library will sponsor a *Week Without Television*. The library will also produce a series of bibliographies that lead readers deeper into the collection. A task force should be assigned the job of creating a series of book discussion programs.

IV.   The good news is that our kids, especially the junior high crowd, goes to the library. The bad news is that we have to do something with them when they get there.

Goal: To provide an after school learning environment.

Objective: Involve 50 percent of the town's junior high school students in after school programs.

Deadline: End of year three.

By refurbishing the basement store room as a quiet study area, and, working with the junior high teachers, set up a homework help program. We can keep the kids tuned into learning and the noise level down to a dull roar.

Follow-Up

Much can change in the course of five years. The Board of Trustees and the Library Director should, on an annual basis, review progress towards the goals that we have outlined here. As the need arises, they could also review the assumptions we have made, and revise the plan to meet the contemporary situation.

The public is invited to comment on this report. Please direct your questions and suggestions to those listed below. The Planning Committee will be presenting this report to the Board at the February Trustees' meeting (February 15, 6:30, at the library). This meeting is open to all.

Philip Tullberg
Secretary, Planning Committee/Library Director
876-3400

Joan Myers
Chair, Planning Committee/Trustee
876-9542 (w)

Walter Woodward
Chair, Danville Library Board of Trustees
876-1968 (h)

Appendix A

Danville Public
Library Statistics

	1991	**1992**	**1993**
Registered borrowers	5863	5872	5879
Population	9024	9068	9068
Borrowers as % of Population	64.9	64.7	64.8
Circulation	77,370	10,368	113,380
Circulation/capita	8.57	11.6	12.5
Reference	7228	8110	7814
Reference/capita	.80	.861	.861
Program attendance	1828	3526	2327
Program/capita	.202	.388	.256
Number of vol's	36,402	41,343	44,824
Turnover	2.12	2.54	2.52

10 LIVING WITH THE PLAN

Before disbanding the planning committee, review the planning process. At the last meeting, ask the members of the committee to evaluate the planning process. What did they like? What didn't they like? What did they find useful? If they had to do it all over again, what would they do differently? Incorporate their suggestions into the next round of planning, five years hence.

REVIEW THE PLAN

Once or twice a year, the director and the trustees should evaluate the library's progress. At this annual/semi annual review ask:

- Did the library meet the objectives outlined in the plan?

- Has the library been consistently acceding its objectives? Does the library consistently fall short of its objectives? Should we be aiming higher, or scaling back our expectations?

- Has there been a major change in the community that requires us to revise our plans?

If you don't complete an objective by the deadline, push it back. Take some more time. Don't give up on it.

If something really isn't working, don't continue to beat your head against a wall. By all means, keep trying new and different approaches to the problem, but, know that you may have to walk away. There may not be a way to interest young adults in what the library has to offer.

On the other hand, if you have a resounding success, keep at it, follow up, expand the program, and be sure to let people know that great things are happening at the library. Learn from your successes as well as your mistakes.

Look for tools that will help you implement the plan. Look for opportunities to exploit to the library's advantage. Be willing to shift priorities as circumstances change.

Keep talking to people—library users, nonusers, as well as the users of other libraries. What do they like? What do they dislike? Have they seen the library's new parking lot? Do they like the expanding summer hours? Have they noticed an improvement in reference service?

Keep people informed. A mailing list and a newsletter are important tools for keeping in touch with people. Be sure to add the name of anyone who has expressed an interest in the library to the mailing list (even if they called to complain).

Pull out the mission statement from time to time and talk about it. Everyone, the staff, trustees and the director should continue to ask, "What is our business?" and "Who are our customers?" Listen carefully to your customers. Give them what they want and what they need.

There you have it: a plan for your library. All that remains is to go out, and, in the words of an athletic shoe maker, *Just Do It!*

INDEX